Hags

THE TRUE STORY
OF A LIFE LIVED
DURING AND AFTER
THE TIMES
THAT STIRRED
A NATION

by
Joseph Ross

THE TRUE STORY OF A LIFE LIVED
DURING AND AFTER THE TIMES
THAT STIRRED A NATION

by Joseph Ross

Published by Joseph Ross
Minneapolis, MN   U.S.A

All the stories in this book are based on actual experiences.
Some of the names and details have been changed to protect the privacy of the people involved.

Design & Production: Barbara L. Frank
Photography: Maria Midtlyng, (Free People Photography)

Printed in the United States of America
First Edition: First Printing
ISBN: 978-1-61658-739-0
U.S. Library of Congress Case No.: 1-283041451

ALSO BY JOSEPH ROSS
Blue Collar Buddha's: Working Class Wisdom
Shell Shocked: My Family's Story

Dedication

This book is dedicated to the men and women who served our country honorably during it's times of conflict and those who returned home as psychological casualties of those wars. Many were broken and damaged physically, emotionally and spiritually from the injuries of a bloodless wound known as Post Traumatic Stress Disorder.

PTSD is a psychological and emotional tormentor that is permanent in nature, and improvement, in many cases, is not expected. From January through Mid-November of 2009, Combat related PTSD has contributed to the suicides of 140 Soldiers and Marines.

This book took thirteen months to write. Coincidentally, that was the same amount of time for a tour of duty in Vietnam. This was the last page I wrote and it brought me to tears when I noticed that I had completed it on Veterans Day, November 11, 2009 at 11:50 pm.

Joseph Ross

I love working and hanging out with all types of creative people, especially those in the hair business. Having a good time just being myself and helping others is my drug of choice these days. Besides hair and books, I have a passion for motorcycles and sports cars. To keep myself in shape I practice Shotokan karate and I am a second degree black belt. To relax I enjoy soft music, meditation and reading Tarot cards for my friends at home or at the local coffee house. What's important to me is being with people and doing the things I feel moved by. I consider it a blessing to know that I am never alone during the dramas and sitcoms of life's stories. We all have our own beauty and our own beast that we must learn to coexist with.

A Note To My Readers

W hen I began writing this story there was always one question that stood out from the rest. My family and friends wanted to know why I chose "*Hags*" as a title to crown the cover of my new book. I could have come back on them with a "Why not *Hags*?" response, but it wouldn't have answered a good question or satisfied the curiosity that surrounded it. Besides, with my gang at home I couldn't have gotten away with it anyway.

Choosing a name for my book was a lot like the process of getting a new tattoo. It had to have meaning, in a personal way, that I could relate to. One day I was just pondering some ideas that could serve as a title and all of a sudden, like magic, it happened. A voice in my head whispered "*Hags*". It had a catchy sound that I liked so I went with it, but it wasn't until I completed writing this story that I knew why.

There was a time in my life when I saw and experienced the world as a very ugly and vicious place. My life was full of anxiety and frustration. Everything I did was in vain and I didn't have a snowball's chance in hell of gratifying a single desire. It was like, how long was I gonna have to say please before I found some peace? "*Hags*" felt like the word that fit and described my place in the world during those times. It was evil, scary and cruel.

Eventually I emerged from that darkness and found an angel of light who brought me out of that Hell and taught me how to live again. Thank you, Dr. Hanson.

Acknowledgments

L et's start with my wife, Nancy. She's the best deal I ever made in my life. She is a person who cultivates the things she would like to see manifest in her life and contributed a great deal of help in creating this book. Thanks, Nance!

I would like to extend a very special thank you to Lawerence Mize, a life-long friend of mine and a Vietnam Veteran. "Who's Left to Pray" and "The 2 A.M. Blues" are two poems from his book *"Dead Men Calling"* that Larry was kind enough to allow me to share with you.

The presence of my children, Ashley and Jack, along with our Golden Retriever, Riley, who have added so much to my life in so many ways.

The customers and staff of Bruegger's Bagels in Plymouth, MN; especially to Randy, David, Karen, Tina and Jaqi.

I would like to thank the kind folks from Beaver's Pond Press, especially Milt and Amy, for their guidance and interest in me as an aspiring writer.

A special thanks to my writing coach, Beth Beaty, who helped me discover my own way of writing this story.

It was a lot of fun working with my photographer, Maria Midtlyng, (Free People Photography) so I decided to let her create her own acknowledgment for this book. "I use my photography as a way of exploration. Being given the opportunity to work in the creative visuals for "Hags" has been a great experience in just that."

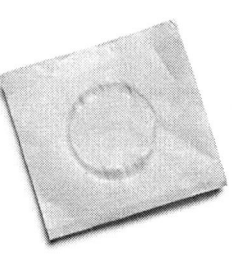

Table Of Contents

Introduction 1

Chapter 1: Greyhound 3

Shunned 13

Chapter 2: Exodus 15

Chapter 3: The Gypsy Trip Doctor 26

2 A.M. Blues 31

Chapter 4: Chronic Déjà vu 32

Who's Left To Pray 41

Chapter 5: Coins 42

Chapter 6: The Rehab Grad 53

Chapter 7: The House 62

Chapter 8: School Circle 74

Chapter 9: Hairballs 85

Chapter 10: Riff Raff's Revenge 96

Chapter 11: Scoundrels, Trophy Wives, and Creep Cheats 111

Chapter 12: Callings 125

Afterward 139

Special Acknowledgement 144

Introduction

Hello. I would like to introduce myself and turn you on to my new book "Hags". I will confess that in birth I entered this world as a bastard and a rebel as well. I make no apology nor do I bear any conflict for that which could not have been avoided because it is the essential nature of a creative artist so I embraced it. My name is Joe and I began writing "Hags" on my fifty-eighth birthday, but this story really began when I was sixteen.

Like most folks, particularly Baby Boomers, I have lived in many parts of the country and I have even left my boot prints on a few parts of the globe, mostly in the middle of a few rice paddies in the darkness while quietly watching and waiting. Other times, my boot prints may have been seen while entering and leaving a village whorehouse when I needed the touch and warmth of another human being that let me know that I was still alive. It was gas, grass or ass because nobody rode free, at least not here.

During the course of my life I've worn many hats, and even a few helmets along the way.

I know that shit happens because I've done my share of burning and crawling through enough of it. I have also learned that it's possible to come out of the other end looking and smelling like a white rose that was ready for change and freedom.

The stories in this book are true because I lived, experienced, and survived them. Often the calm between the storms was filled with beer, cigarettes, weed, and perhaps a letter from anybody back in the world. Anything was better than the uncertainty of not knowing what shit was coming next for me. Could I have done without these times that some call the way of the cross? Yeah! But, I would not have become the person I am today.

I would love to tell you about a few of the places I have been. So what do you say? Are you ready for a real ride with some parties and a few adventures while we're at it? I'll take that smile on your face and the gleam in your eyes as a yes!

Cool! Click your heels and hold on because we're going out there. I can't promise you'll return the way you were before we left, but I can promise I'll get you back home one way or another.

Chapter 1: Greyhound

I wasn't sure how to begin this story because it's been almost forty two years since it began. I seem to recall that a Buddhist monk once said "May you live in interesting times". I would like to thank him for that blessing because I believe I have. Sometimes I wonder, could this have been a prophecy predicting one of the most challenging of times for a generation we call The Baby Boomers? This only makes sense when you consider we're the offspring of an era known as The Greatest Generation. They were a tough act to follow and how in the hell do you compete with a curtain call like that?

Believe me we tried. We even started with giving away free love and peace signs. We were on a roll so we dropped out, tuned in and turned on. We were breaking new ground while living in communes and the theme of our collective consciousness was never to trust anyone over thirty. I would have to say that we had some first class acts. We even took center stage for awhile, but no matter how hard we tried we could never grasp superstardom. That prize had been given to those who had come before us. Because of their courage and sacrifice, we were able to grow up in a great country and enjoy life in some the best of times.

This chapter of "*Hags*" is in no way a history lesson of the old knowledge or the ancient wisdom of a middle aged fart like me. "*Hags*" does have it's beginning during the age of Aquarius, the Sexual Revolution and the Vietnam War. Perhaps it would be better said that old knowledge and ancient wisdom are constantly renewed, ever changing and growing.

I was a young pup back then, frisky, snappy and cute. I guess I can chuckle about that because puppies usually are. When I look in a mirror today the reflection shows an older hound who still has his teeth and hair while contemplating on the things that matter in my life now. Older men and puppies are cute, although we may leave the seat up and wet the floor, and may even look and behave like bulldogs in the morning. Our jaws may tend to drop - it's just one of those things that come with age. I'm not as snappy anymore because life has been a good trainer and I've learned over the years there's no need to be. I may be a hound but I've always known that my ancestors were wolves, and becoming a hunter was a skill that came naturally for me.

I guess some things never change, like the memories and feelings that have long since passed but are never gone. As I sat down and began writing this book they returned once more just to bite my ass again in a way that was very familiar. In less time than it has taken you to read this page, I felt an intense stare returning to my eyes again. That old feeling of a calm, but steady, intention within my body that was ready to act and do whatever was necessary in the moment without any hesitation. My breathing has stopped for a few seconds now. This means I have just sent a rifle round on it's way to do what I can't imagine and I don't think I want to know.

This chapter is titled "Greyhound" but it's not about the breed of a dog. This story is about the men who became the dogs of war and with whom I served with as a member of the pack…The few, the proud, the brave, the Marines. By the time this war is over a few will be all that's left to tell the stories about so many who died fighting their way back home. I sure wish I could've written about how we lived and returned as heroes with lots of smiles and cheers, and shaking hands and kissing babies but it didn't happen that way. The great homecoming party we were all looking forward to never happened either, at least not for most of us. Looking back, it was nothing more than wishful thinking and fantasizing. If there wasn't a send off party when we left why would there be one for a job well done when we returned. The Drill

Instructors at Parris Island told us not to worry about smoking cigarettes and lung cancer. It was a waste of time because Marines never lived long enough to develop cancer. That turned out to become a harsh truth for me. Within a year, half of us would be dead or severely wounded. Those of us that depression and suicide didn't kill, alcoholism and Agent Orange related cancers did. Some of us drank to forget and others because they were still scared. I did both, and a few other things along the way. I ended up living between my mother's house and a few homeless shelters - sometimes she just couldn't deal with my issues. I remember believing that all I had to do was to get out of Vietnam alive and the rest of my life would be gravy. What the hell was I thinking? There wasn't any gravy before Vietnam. Why would there be any when I got home?

I had more shit to deal with in my life after Vietnam than I had ever experienced before going. I had to find a way to live with this until my world took a new turn. I did whatever I had to do to buy time and sometimes that meant selling my own blood. The city blood bank would pay between fifteen to twenty five dollars for a pint of blood. I had A+, the cheap stuff. It was good for fifteen bucks. If you had that rare stuff in your veins, the price went up to twenty five. Not all blood banks and plasma centers were the same. Some paid more than others and if you lucked out finding a research project at a private center you could make the big bucks - fifty to one hundred dollars easy for one pint of blood. I guess it was a good idea to let your fingers do the walking before your arm exposed it's vein. I got in and out of the blood bank as fast as I could because I never cared much for the waiting area. It was full of a lot of people like me who were down and out, broke and embarrassed, due to situations that were sometimes beyond our control. Whoever said "misery loves company" was a fucking liar. I don't remember ever seeing anybody who was happy to be there.

During the lean times, when I couldn't spare the blood or the plasma, my television and I had a business relationship with Eddie Katz, owner of the local pawn shop. That guy helped me out a lot.

He was always willing to front me fifty bucks while holding onto my TV until the first of the month when I got paid.

When I wasn't in a Veterans Administration Rehab Center, I was on the Maryland welfare system, known as Social Services. The welfare department gave me $120 a month to rent a sleeping room in West Baltimore and $40 in food stamps. I was a late night shopper because I didn't want anyone to know that I was on food stamps. The extra money I got from the blood bank and the pawn shop kept me in cigarettes, health and hygiene items, and some cheap shit to drink. Anything that wasn't nailed down that I could get my hands on ended up hocked or in a junk yard for whatever I could get for it.

I guess it's fair to say that all of us returned home broken and damaged in one way or another. Nobody comes back from a war without something besides a few medals and possibly a case of the clap. Often we refer to ourselves as The Dying Breed because Vietnam was our war, our blood, and our lives. My personal story is how by the grace of God I returned, was healed and learned how to live again.

I needed to write about this war and how I survived it and the people who helped me along the way. I finally returned to a place that made sense and I was no longer afraid of the dark anymore. I no longer sleep with a gun under my pillow, but it's placed on a small table next to my bed. Most wives would consider this a deal breaker, but all I can say is that Nancy understands. She knows in her heart and mind that I could never give up the security of having my weapon close by.

My time in this war started at the Greyhound Bus Terminal in Baltimore, Maryland and began in 1967. Every war needs a few good men. Some were known as writers and some were known as pencil pushing motherfuckers by others. Personally, I'm not here to pen whip anything or anybody - all that matters to me is the truth of this story.

This wasn't the job I had set out to do and it sure as hell wasn't the one the Marines had in mind for me. Let's just say, by fate, it's the one I ended up with. Our country is at war once more and, as usual, it's in a distant place that most of us have never heard of. The timing always sucks for a war and it's always with the wrong people.

My name is Joe.

I'm not a Marine yet, but I'm on my way to become one. A few Greyhounds will be heading south on Highway 95 tonight - I know because I will be on one of them with about fifty other young men. That's the count unless somebody skips out between now and when we get to where we are going. I wouldn't have missed this trip for the world. Speaking of the world, it hasn't changed much since the last three wars. Countries are still screwing their friends and killing their enemies.

The Marines need men to fill it's ranks and when Uncle Sam calls, it's always the boys who answer and show up. That's okay with the Marines because that's the way it's always been.

For the most part, the age gap in this crowd is between seventeen and twenty-one except for me.

I'm still sixteen, but I'll be seventeen in a few weeks. Not too much of a stretch, and who's to know that cares anyway. I lied about my age and I ranted and raved so much at my mother that she finally caved in and signed my enlistment papers. She promised to keep her mouth shut and I promised to send home twenty bucks a month out of my pay to make sure that she did.

I don't mean to disappoint you with some of the knowledge regarding my family background but the only "Leave It To Beaver" family in my neighborhood was on television. I never cared much for the show, and besides, we all knew that Ward Cleaver was always a little hard on the Beaver.

One time when I was fourteen my best friend, Greg Senkus, and I were out on a boating trip around the Chesapeake Bay. As I remember I became very seasick. Too bad, because I think now that's what stopped me from going Navy. My best friend to this day, Greg, never embraced the war but he did participate in peace marches and war rallies. I'm happy that things went that way. It would have been really tough if my life long friend would have been killed in a war that he wanted nothing to do with. It was hard enough on Greg and his family just to know that I was leaving soon.

That doesn't matter for me right now because things are what they are and I'm here for the beginning of a war that is going to last for a very long time. Every war starts with a time and place where guys like me form up. Sometimes it's an airport, often a train station, but no such luck for me and the others tonight. We're going via Greyhound Bus Lines from Baltimore all the damn way to Parris Island, South Carolina. By the time we get there it's going to feel more like a ride on a cattle car than on a bus. I hope they plan on feeding us along the way. I've only got twenty bucks to my name and I would like to hold onto it as long as I can. The Greyhound might be a dogs way of getting around but it was one of the Corps. best friends and has taken Marine Corps. recruits to Parris Island for the last three wars now.

There's always plenty of foot traffic in a Greyhound bus terminal, especially during a war. Plenty of people coming and going, and some who are never coming back. In the center of the terminal I saw a blind man selling cigarettes and candy from a kiosk. My first thought was "How in the hell does this guy not get ripped off?" I watched him for a few minutes and I noticed he was truly a class act even though he was blind as a bat. When it came to passing cash his fingers possessed an acute sensitivity. He knew the value of currency simply by the way it felt and returned the correct change due to a customer as well.

Even the cops had something to do here besides enjoying the free coffee and donuts. They just removed a couple of drunks who were working the crowd for some spare change. I bet by the end of the night they had enough to cover a round at the tavern across the street. The cops weren't really hard on these guys. They just wanted them out of the terminal for the comfort of the passengers.

I ended up speaking with a flower child for a few minutes, at least that's what I thought she was because of the patch on her jacket telling people to smile because this was the first day of the rest of their life. With her long blond hair and a Jimi Hendrix bandana around her head she fit the part. She walked up and hit on me for a few cigarettes so I gave her what was left of an open pack. It was going to be a long time before I had the chance to speak with a girl again, so I made the most of it. I asked her where she was going and she said "Nowhere. My Dad is coming to pick me up". I told her I was on my way to Parris Island to become a Marine. She said "That's sad, but good luck anyway. Thank you for the cigarettes." Then she just walked out the door.

I don't care so much for the word terminal anymore because it just feels so personal to me now. The guy on the intercom here sure is loud and clear about arrivals and departures. He's always repeating things twice. I think he might be a little anal about his job. I can tell that some of these guys I'm with don't want to leave and others, like me, can't bear to stay. I never had much while I was growing up so I guess I won't miss as much now that I'm leaving.

Most of us are Catholic Irish guys from West Baltimore, with one or two years of high school at the most. I dropped out of school in the ninth grade, but I'm street smart as hell and that's good enough for where I am going. It sounds like that asshole on the intercom is at it again. What a prick! Just when I was going to get a cup of coffee and have a smoke he ends up blowing it for me. "Attention, Attention Please! All Marine Corps. recruits for Parris Island, South Carolina please board now on buses number twenty three and twenty five. I repeat, please begin boarding now and thank you for going Greyhound." Well, this is it, my ride is here and in a matter of hours life as I know it will change completely.

I know that eventually we will be going into harms way but right now I just want to enjoy the ride. I find the conversations and the jokes we share across the aisles are funny and interesting. I'm sure there's nothing we could say or do that our driver hasn't seen or heard a hundred times before as our bus heads down the road. Most of the guys smoke cigarettes, including me, but what really blows my mind is all the bullshit about getting laid before leaving home. If I didn't know any better, this crowd would have me believing that getting laid was a prerequisite before enlisting into the Marine Corps. Perhaps I better keep my mouth shut just in case it is.

Most of us can't believe we are going to get three meals a day. I've never had three meals in a single day in my life! Two maybe, but never three. We never had enough money to afford three meals a day, seven days a week, when I was growing up. The thought of having three meals a day sounded too good to be true. The Marines call it chow. I just called it a bonus.

It was an all night ride to Parris Island but with everybody laying out their best bullshit the time passed quickly. All it takes is a good ice breaker and before you know it everyone's a comedian. We get gabby as hell. We all had stories about the first time we got drunk and how we fell to our knees before that porcelain God. And then there were the things you never tell a best friend, like how you got a hard-on for his mother the first time you met her or how you made out with his girlfriend behind the bleachers when he was on the field playing football.

This was the kind of funny shit that happened that all of us could relate to as young men.

As the bus passed through the gate and I saw the yellow footprints just outside the window, I knew the party was over for a long time to come. When the bus stopped and the doors opened that's when the hell began. A Drill Instructor jumped on the bus and started screaming at us to get our fucking asses off the bus now while two other Drill Instructors outside of the bus were screaming "Move it, move it, move it. Get your fucking feet on the yellow footprints now and keep 'em there. Don't eyeball my fucking area. You don't deserve to step foot on my island. That's why you are standing on the yellow footprints. Those yellow footprints are there for you to stand on and pray.

Let God know that you have given him your soul because your ass now belongs to me." I had no idea how long we stood there with those three Drill Instructors screaming at us all at the same time. I had gotten lost in the craziness that was surrounding us now. I remember our driver saying just before he closed the door, "Thank you for going Greyhound". When that bus pulled away and left us, I remember thinking to myself...Welcome to the Marine Corps.

When a Drill Instructor screams at you with a war face the color of blood and warns you not to screw up again, he means it. When he threatens to tear off your head and shit down your throat it gets your attention real fast. A recruit could get slapped silly just for eyeballing the area while a Drill Instructor was talking. If a Drill Instructor wasn't making your life miserable enough you can bet the heat, humidity and sand fleas would pick up where he left off.

I knew that Parris Island was going to be hard and it sure as hell was. We started with eighty recruits and after the first two weeks we were down to sixty. Some of these guys had bad hearts and didn't know it and others were non-hackers, including a few who may have played the homo card. I guess life just had a different plan for these guys we call Baby Blue Marines. Just like farmers who stay home to grow crops and take care of the land, maybe these guys were needed to stay home and create families and raise kids. With the unrest and discontent this war has placed on our country and many of its people, maybe these guys just might restore a sense of balance and harmony from what this war has taken away. I would like to believe that their failure now will somehow serve a greater purpose later on. After all, isn't this what we were fighting for? Life, liberty, and justice, and let's not forget those who were not able to fight for themselves. The Corps. shit-canned them and sent 'em home. The rest of us hung in there and made it, and after three months we were now United States Marines.

On graduation day we proudly marched in formation while

shouldering our rifles and following the cadence commands of our Drill Instructors on the parade field for our families and sweethearts that had come to honor our achievement. We were given four hours of base liberty that day to spend with our family and friends. Can you believe the next morning a Greyhound bus was outside the barracks waiting to take us to Camp LeJeune for six weeks of Advanced Infantry Training. This time getting on the bus was a lot easier than it was getting off the bus when we first arrived. The Drill Instructors were no longer calling us scumbags, shit birds, motherfuckers, and ladies. They were now shaking each one of our hands as we boarded that damn bus again with the same old driver, saying "Well done, Marine".

After grunt training at LeJeune and a ten day leave to go home to visit my family and kick back for a much needed break, I was given orders to report to the 5th Marine Division at Camp Pendleton, California. Hanging out with my fellow Jarheads in Oceanside strip joints and laying out on the beaches surrounded by plenty of eye candy became a cozy scene. Life was good until the Marines felt I could use a new friend so they issued me one, an M14-7.62 mm rifle and it wasn't long before I got to know it real well. Soon my rifle and I were real buddy-buddy and became the best of friends. My trigger finger was so sensitive that I could warm up the coldest nipple on a witch's tit with a single touch.

The Marine Corps. noticed real fast that I had a soft touch for the things they considered very important so they sent me to a place where they felt that I would be warmly received. The Black Pearl of the Orient, also known as Vietnam, to spend some quality time with the 1st Marine Division in the tropical Central Highlands.

What can I say? I was just another boot that had been screwed again by the green weenie and I wasn't even given the courtesy of a reach-around.

Shunned

Once I dreamed about a hallway that was long and full of doors.

It was white and brightly lit with a shiny crystal floor.

I stood before a doorway and a gentle voice called out my name

"Joseph, would you please come in and spend some time with me?"

Jesus Christ was at a table and he asked me to sit down.

I said, "Thank you, Lord, could we have a drink because

this is my first time here in town."

Jesus looked straight at me and asked if I knew his name.

I said, "Yes Lord, you know I do. I've used it many times in vain."

We sat awhile in silence as his presence touched my soul,

but when he looked into my heart, hell's darkness was exposed.

It must have really freaked him out because

he whispered slowly that he had to let me go.

I was not surprised. This was just the same old shit
that he pulled all the time.

"I'm not the first or the last that you have left behind.

I'm sorry that I burdened you thinking you were on my side."

Ring around the rosey,

A pocketful of posies.

Ashes, ashes.

We all fall down.

Chapter 2: Exodus

March, 1969
Hill 10, a Marine fire base in the Central Highlands of Vietnam

I t's another hot day in this shit hole of a place. I can use that term because I have done my share of burning it with diesel fuel from underneath the latrines. Screwing something up usually granted me the privilege of burning shit. That's okay, I was never alone. The heat only adds to the misery of being here.

When I arrived here I was young and exploring much of the world for the first time. My cup wasn't empty but it was small and needed to grow. My first thought about Vietnam was "God, does this place suck." It was hot, humid, dusty and sweaty, but after awhile I got used to it. Vietnam gave me a real perspective of what sucked in the world and what didn't.

I'm on Hill 10 with the 1st Marines in the Central Highlands about fifteen miles SW of Da Nang. I've been here for a few months and I'm still considered an FNG (Fucking New Guy) by the short timers. I have a lot of respect for these guys but I feel like I'm trying to find my way here and nobody feels like I'm worth enough to explain the rules to yet. It's hard to connect with people when you feel they don't want you around. I stay as close to these men as I possibly can. I need to learn everything from them about how to survive here before they return back to the world. It's not what you do out here that matters, but how long you live to do it that counts. Getting out of Vietnam requires two things, learning how to survive and luck.

So far my combat experience against the enemy has been deadly.

I've managed to kill at least a hundred bugs and some of the biggest rats I've ever seen in my life. The Marine Corps. should award me the Purple Heart for all the bug bites I've suffered alone. I have one confirmed kill for my service record book. It was a skinny dog from a nearby village that scared the shit out of me. I was walking perimeter guard in the fog when it happened. I'm sure it was a Gook's dog so maybe that should count for something.

I'm here, the war is here and Vietnam is here. I'm so angry now as I look around this place. I can't see anything worth fighting for except each other. I've never seen a place with as many holes in the earth as I've seen here. If it's not one we've dug with our sand shovels, it's a crater that was left behind from an NVA rocket.

We're here fighting for the hearts and minds of a people and it's culture that we don't know jack shit about. I guess I'm supposed to believe that inside of every Gook there's an American waiting to jump out. With that thought, maybe we'll have more admirers than we have enemies now. What I hate about the South Vietnamese soldiers isn't that they can't fight for their country, but that they won't. Their personal truth is that they don't believe in what they are fighting for. They haven't learned yet that freedom isn't free so they try to comp a free ride by having us do their fighting for them. If I die here I just hope it's not in a hole with one of them. It's bad enough that I have to eat chow with these shit birds.

The North Vietnamese, on the other side of the coin, are fighting to reclaim their land and unify their country once more. The North Vietnamese soldiers believe they were born in the north to die in the south. Ho Chi Min said "This has now become an American war. We will lose many and they will lose few. Soon they will tire and go home." I believe he may have been telling the truth because many of us who were born in the west will end up dying here in the east.

Time in Vietnam is slow time and I do whatever I can to keep my mind occupied. I don't know what day it is and I'm not sure what month it is either. To know the day and month is a luxury for the short timers who will be going back to the world soon. I'm still so new here I am lucky to have a watch, a broken one at that. I wear it for luck. The time says 6:30 on it. So what if it is a broken watch? The value to me is that it lets me know twice a day that I am still alive.

Any place in this country, at any given time, can be just as different as night and day, and just as two sided. The 1st Marines are kicking ass and taking names during the day, but we all know that Charlie owns the night. There are three things I can say for sure about the North Vietnamese Army. They don't run, they're not afraid to fight, and none of them are cowards. Then again, it's easy to be brave when you haven't got a choice. They know that whenever we find them they have become dead men walking. That's why we call it "search and destroy". They don't take prisoners and sometimes as payback, neither do we.

Charlie hit us last night big time. Mortars and RPG's came in just as I started reading a letter from home. I grabbed my helmet and rifle and ran like a bat out of hell for a bunker. When I was about half way to the bunker I saw a huge explosion high above the ground. One of our towers had taken a direct hit from an RPG. A red and orange fireball exploded and the tower was gone. By the time we started shooting back it was over. That's when the yelling started "Corpsman, Corpsman" and after that came the screaming and the cursing.

There's a lot of confusion going on right now because so much is happening and we don't know how many casualties we have taken. The sirens are still going and a few of our hootches have been blown up. Our Corpsmen have to keep our seriously wounded alive until a Medevac chopper arrives, and that means ain't nobody getting out 'til daylight. I just hope a Huey makes it in and out as soon as possible for our wounded and our dead.

My heart is beating so fast even though things are quieting down. We have three dead from the lookout tower and Andy has a small scratch on his nose. It's bleeding some. Looks like a piece of shrapnel grazed it. Lucky! He'll get a Purple Heart for that and three days at China Beach. I just jumped back in a bunker again. There's no light and it's pitch black inside of here. I need to stay until somebody calls out my name. I just want to sit on my ass in the dark and smoke a few cigarettes. I wish I could fall asleep for just a few hours and not get bit by a rat or some kind of goddamned bug, for that matter. No, I don't want to know what day, night or month it is. I do know it's 6:30 twice a day, one day at a time on this broken ass watch, and like I said before that's twice a day I know I'm still alive. I pray that things that are broken will still have some value some place. I hope so, because after this war is over a lot of us are not coming home as one solid piece, not after all of this. Many will be broken and damaged.

I see the Vietnamese people only as objects to be used, with no regard for their own well being, and of which I feel a deep contempt for. Right now nothing outside of me is as important as what is going on inside of me. The sights and sounds of war in this country are the same and the feeling of fresh grief is always in the air. I guess it is one of those mind over matter things. The truth is that I don't mind because they don't matter.

Every day that I am here I see the writing on the wall and it's not just graffiti anymore, but an outcry of the truth. This isn't our war, it's theirs, and we don't belong here. We're fighting for the hearts and minds of others while ignoring the truth and soul of our own. There's no lack of pretension here in Vietnam. I feel like it's one big whore house on the map and we're the johns that are being taken for everything they can get out of us. I don't believe our message of freedom and the pursuit of happiness has been delivered to the correct people or received in the spirit it was intended. It doesn't really matter what the truth is anymore. The only domino effect I see in Vietnam is our own falling in a fixed game. If we're here to fight this war under a false pretense, so be it. My loyalty is to the Marine Corps. and I will fight on that lie, if need be.

A lot of us have only been out of high school a year and here we are in Vietnam. Young men have died here without ever knowing the experience of passion with a woman. Roughly about seventy percent of the Marines who were here when I arrived are gone. About half of them finished their tour of duty and were rotated back to the States. Our wounded were sent to hospital ships off of the coast, and later were transferred to Naval hospitals in the States to be treated and discharged, for the most part. Our fallen Marines were embalmed at Da Nang and flown to Hawaii, where they were dressed in Blues and sent home in government issued coffins to be received by their families.

Most of the new replacements are FNG's and I don't know any of them. I'm just sick and tired of all their stupid questions. Questions like "How often do we get hit?" All I can say is "You'll know when we do." I have only been here a few months and I'm not even eighteen years old yet. Maybe I should be telling these guys that you can vanish like a fart in the wind here and the next day no one will even remember your name. When I think about it, I don't feel much like a new guy anymore.

Besides Charlie trying to put my dick in the dirt, I've got some new problems of my own now. A few times this week, for no reason at all, my heart started beating really fast and I was hyperventilating at the same time. Both of my arms would go cold and numb. Just before this happens, a feeling of deep fear would come over my entire body. It felt like something unknown and deep inside was pulling me away against my will. Everything outside of me was fading away and I couldn't stop it. I feared my own death was occurring now and part of me was dying from the inside out. It also happened again just before I was going out on perimeter guard. Two Marines I was with thought I was having a heart attack and carried me to the Corpsman's bunker. Our Corpsman gave me oxygen and a shot to relax me, and in a few hours I was fine.

I've been to the Corpsman twice for this now and in a few days I am going to Division Rear in Da Nang to see a doctor and get checked out. Whatever this is has me scared. I can't do my job and I'm on light duty until I get back from Da Nang. Another thing is I can't can't piss either. Everything is just frozen and I'm in a lot of discomfort from having a full bladder that seldom releases itself and I am extremely bloated.

Our Corpsman gave me some pills to help me relax until I can see the Doc in Da Nang. I don't know what they are but they seem to help some. I seldom get any sleep here and when I do my nightmares are unimaginable. Upon awakening and finding myself here I experience the nightmare as a reality. One night I dreamt that I was shot and killed by an NVA soldier while I was coming out of a bunker. I saw myself dead on an embalming table. I was floating above my body and could see everything the embalmer was doing to me. I could feel the cool wetness of the formaldehyde as it passed through my veins. I remember screaming at the mortician to stop because I was still alive, but he couldn't hear me and continued his work. I saw that my fate was hopeless and that I had power over nothing. This is just one of the many nightmares I experienced in Vietnam as my condition worsened.

I've noticed our Corpsman has been keeping an eye on me and that, in itself, has made me somewhat nervous. Speaking of nervous, Oh, shit! Here comes Mr. Righteous Anger himself, Gunnery Sergeant Jones, and he doesn't look happy. "Ross!"

"Yeah, Gunny"

"Jesus, Joseph, and doggy style Mary. What is your major malfunction today Marine? Captain Taylor has ordered me to transport you to Division Rear Medical in Da Nang ASAP. You don't look sick, lame, lazy or crazy to me. If this is some kind of stunt to get you a three day R & R, I promise I'll hang your ass when you get back. Now saddle up and grab your war gear and get going. And Ross..."

"Yeah, Gunny?"

"When you get back you best have your head and ass wired together or I'll have you burning shit and filling sandbags for the rest of this god damn war, do you hear me?"

"Yeah, thanks, Gunny. See you soon." I grabbed my helmet, flack jacket and M-14, jumped into the back of a Jeep with a driver and another Marine who was riding shotgun. We were locked, loaded and gone.

That was the last time I would ever see any of the men I had served with again. Unbeknownst to me, this was my last ride here in this country as a combat Marine and I was leaving Vietnam. I was a casualty of this war and I didn't even know it.

It was a short ride from Hill 10 to the Naval treatment center in Da Nang, less than an hour. There wasn't much conversation going on in the Jeep. We were crossing a lot of open country and had to pay attention to our surroundings. Soon we arrived at the treatment center and I checked in my weapon before entering the medical facility. I gave my papers to a clerk and was told to have a seat and that a doctor would see me soon. I sat across from a Marine whose flack jacket was still bloody. It was his friend's blood, who had been shot earlier by a sniper, and he brought him here to the aid station for care. He looked at me and started crying because he couldn't believe this had just happened to one of his close friends. The only thing I was able to say was that I was very sorry. I couldn't say anything else because there were no words left inside of me to say.

After a couple of hours a door opened and a Naval doctor said, "Ross will you come in please". I took a seat after I closed the door behind me. I could tell from the look on his face that something was up. After he finished reviewing my medical record and gave me a brief physical examination he asked how I was feeling now. I said "I don't know, Sir. How do you think this thing is going to go?" And he answered, "Not well for you."

"Sir, is there a problem with my heart that is creating the rapid beating I've had to deal with?"

"No, Ross, your heart is fine but you have other concerns that need to be addressed."

I asked him what those concerns were and he replied "Ross, I'm sorry that I have to tell you this, but I believe that you are a psychological casualty of this war. In fact, I'm ordering that you be hospitalized now and Medevaced back to the States as soon as possible."

I said "No doc, you're wrong". I jumped to my feet and prepared to return to my unit.

"No son, you're not returning to your unit. I can't allow you to do that".

As I continued to de-ass the area, I was restrained by a few Corpsmen, given a shot of something and I fell into unconsciousness. I remember waking up from time to time while I was on an Air Force medical evacuation jet and saw that it was full of severely wounded casualties. I recall seeing another Marine on a stretcher with part of his skull missing. The killing had ended but the process of death was still taking place. Marines on this jet were dying now as I was lying here in my own urine and feces, with leather restraints around my arms and ankles. I remember screaming as a nurse gave me another shot to knock me out again. GOD, YOU CAN'T SEND ME HOME THIS WAY! I CAN'T COME HOME THIS WAY!

I always figured if I got killed here I would have never known what had hit me, and knowing that was always my comfort. I had no idea that part of me was already gone and how true it was that I had never known what had hit me nor that I would coexist with the reality of this nightmare for the rest of my life.

I don't remember much about that flight back because I was heavily sedated, and maybe it's a good thing that I didn't. I swear, every time I woke up a nurse gave me a shot that knocked my ass out again. When we got to the States I was hospitalized at St. Albans Naval Hospital in New York.

Soon the medical staff saw there was no need for the restraints so they were removed and I was confined to a locked down ward for observation. This part of the hospital was full of drug addicts from all branches of the service that had come back from Vietnam. There were some real nuts in here and a few catatonic patients as well. Even though I was screwed up, big time on Thorazine, my thoughts were clear that I was none of the above, so why the fuck was I here? I spent two weeks in that hell hole before I was moved to an open ward. I was angry as hell because I knew that I didn't belong here. The doctors at St. Albans kept me medicated on Thorazine, which I hated! It made me drool from my mouth like some kind of goddamned dog.

If I tried to walk very fast, my heart rate would uncomfortably speed up. One side effect of the Thorazine was diarrhea, and I learned that I could never trust a fart.

After a few weeks of Thorazine, playing cards, television, and sleeping I was called in for a medical review. This review was to determine if I could possibly return to active duty or be discharged. A few days later I was ordered to speak with a young First Lieutenant Naval Officer by the name of Dr. Hanson. I had met with him a few times in the treatment center, but never in his office. One thing I remembered about this doctor was his lab coat. It was the most starched out, bleached out lab coat I had ever seen. I knocked on his door and he looked up and said "Come in Ross and have a seat. I have your paperwork here from the Review Board and I'm afraid you're not going to like what it has to say. We know you requested a return to duty but after a careful review of your case, I'm afraid that won't be possible. It has been concluded, because of your condition, that you are of no use to the Marine Corps. You will be given an honorable discharge today and you will be released from the United States Marine Corps."

I sat there for a moment thinking and asked if there was anything I could do. He answered "Yes, go home and live your life the best way you can".

"Doc, you can't do this to me. What do I have left without the Corps?"

"I'm sorry son, but I have to let you go".

I was honorably discharged from St. Albans Naval Hospital in New York, given a bus ticket and twenty one dollars in cash. Because my pay record was still in Vietnam the military would not advance me even a dollar more. Other than my mother's house I had no place to go, no meds, nobody to turn to and absolutely no idea, other than being declared a psychological casualty of the war, of what was wrong with me.

It seems like it was just yesterday that I was at Parris Island as a recruit and now I was being discharged from a hospital and the Marines. All I could do was pack up my sea bag and leave because I was ordered out. The bus ride from New York back home to Baltimore was lonely and inside I felt empty as hell. I don't remember saying one word or making eye contact with a single passenger that day. Yet, I felt that all eyes were on me as a United States Marine and that I was something special and worthy of respect. I had my ribbons on my chest for my service in Vietnam but it was everything I could do not to break down in front of these people while I was in this uniform. They weren't looking at me but at the uniform that they believed to be what I was. No matter how much pain I was feeling inside, I wasn't going to say or do anything that was unbecoming of a United States Marine.

After a three hour bus ride it ended where it all began, at the Greyhound Bus Terminal in Baltimore. The place looked the same as it did two years ago when I left. I went home to my mother's house and my sister met me at the door. She gave me a long hug and welcomed me home again as I closed the door behind me.

I avoided talking to or seeing anyone I knew, and other than going out for a pack of cigarettes I didn't leave my house for over a year. All I could do was eat, sleep, and smoke cigarettes. I have no idea how I survived that first year, but I did. The next five years of my life were almost as challenging. Some of my lowest times were the relentless continuation of the panic attacks that followed me home from Vietnam. I couldn't work or function as a normal human being anymore, and the thought of suicide seemed to be my only way to escape the constant suffering and the severe depression of my condition.   Because I had refused help from the Veterans Administration, my family felt that they had become over burdened as my caretakers.   Due to the arguments between my mother and myself, I would find myself in homeless shelters from time to time. I was always calling my mother on the phone, begging her to let me come home again and things would be different, but they never were. One day she just couldn't take it anymore and dropped me off at the VA Medical Center in Baltimore, and told me not to call her again until I was well.

I stopped asking myself a long time ago why this had happened to me. In no way, shape or form could I have asked for the healing or the forgiveness of God. I could only curse and blame Him from my knees for the condition I found myself in as a human being because of the faults and failures of my creator himself. In truth, I would have bayoneted the throat of Christ just to have gotten even with God for allowing this condition to have happened to me.

While I have often waited for an answer from inside myself to feel more reassured about what was next for me, never have I experienced one. The only thing I ever found in asking why was self deception. The real truth, no rhyme or reason. Why me? Why not me? It just happened.

Chapter 3: The Gypsy Trip Doctor

November, 1975
Veterans Medical Center, Baltimore, Maryland
Six Years Later

D r. Ted Hanson is driving his silver BMW through the Maryland countryside on his way to work at Veterans Medical Center in Baltimore. He's new to the area and finds the fall colors of the maple and oak trees are beautiful.

While he is listening to Simon and Garfunkel music on his eight track stereo, he finds comfort in the words of the song "That flowers never bend in the rainfall no matter if you're born to play the king or pawn, the line is thinly drawn between joy and sorrow." It's the right time and the right place for Ted Hanson and his family. He has just accepted a residency position at the Veterans Medical Center after spending the last eight years as a therapist at St. Albans Naval Hospital in New York. His work has primarily been focused on the effects of Post Traumatic Stress Disorder on combat psychological casualties of the Vietnam War.

Dr. Hanson has been promoted to Head of Psychiatry for the new Post Traumatic Stress Wing at Veterans Medical Center in Baltimore. His wife's family is from Maryland and they live in a small town by the name of Towson. With the pay increase and a promotion, the move was a good thing.

He could've chosen Sinai Medical Center in New York or even Boston General in Massachusetts. He didn't have to apply because they offered him a blank check just to sign on.

Dr. Hanson's work in Post Traumatic Stress Disorder and Acute

Anxiety Disorder was widely known. His lectures at various universities and medical centers had become noteworthy enough to appear as columns in the Journal of American Medicine and the American Psychiatric Review. PTSD was the new buzz word around town and he was the slick guy who knew the most about it. He could've written his own ticket to any place in the country he wanted to go but instead of taking a joy ride off to a prestigious medical center in a glamorous city elsewhere, he went with his gut. I'd have to put my money on a hunch that he knew guys like me needed him right here in Baltimore.

This was good work for a man as young as he was. I have to admit, I didn't think too much of the man the first time I laid eyes on him but that was my first impression of Ted Hanson many years ago at St. Albans Naval Hospital in New York. A lot of things have come to pass for him since then, but not so much for me. Most things in my life are pretty much the same.

After Vietnam I was deeply depressed and lonely. I avoided relationships with people who were truly capable of taking that away. I would become angry at them as a self defensive way of holding on to what I knew. It was safe because depression was much easier to bear than the pain of additional loss or rejection. This is a common trait of PTSD - with veterans it's known as "bunkering up". I needed help desperately because I had begun planning my next suicide attempt, so I checked myself into the Veterans Medical Center in Baltimore. I never would have guessed that Dr. Ted Hanson was the man who was going to save my ass and teach me how to live again.

Dr. Hanson performed his internship and first residency at St. Albans Naval Hospital. He worked deeply in the field of mental health for over six years after his internship. Dr. Hanson worked with a psychiatric nurse by the name of Ellen Burdick, whom he had met at the beginning of his internship and continued working with during his residency. The two worked well together at St. Albans and after two years found themselves in charge of intake evaluations and the treatment staff. Dr. Hanson very much valued Ellen's dedication and competence at St. Albans. He was also very taken with her sense of commitment and loyalty to him as a subordinate. This shared interest and commonality was a major contributor that made them BFF's (Best Friends Forever). He offered her a promotion and asked if she would consider working with him in Baltimore as Head of Nursing in the Post Traumatic Stress Recovery Unit at Veterans Medical Center.

Ellen and her husband, Tom, had been happily married for over five years. They were in the process of planning a family when Tom tragically died in an automobile accident. Ellen had lost her husband and their plans for a family very suddenly. She was also very passionate about her work with Ted Hanson and in no way was she going to lose them both.

As far as Dr. Hanson was concerned, Ellen was vital to the continuation and success of his work with PTSD. He needed a close associate to work with to continue the experimental work they had been doing with his new Compass of Cognitive Being (COCB) therapy model.

Along with Dr. Hanson, she had discovered many insights about PTSD which helped create a strong foundation for their new therapy model. Together they knew they were on a promising path for the treatment of PTSD and Acute Anxiety Disorder (AAD) as well. She was, without a doubt, the most important member of his research and development team so she readily accepted his proposal and agreed to sign on as his Head of Nursing and personal assistant.

Because of their experience and knowledge of treatment during the trial and error years of working with PTSD, the two of them had developed a reputation of significance in the field and study of Post Traumatic Stress Disorder. This, in turn, placed them as a top choice on a short list of candidates that could lead and direct the new mental health wing at Veterans Medical Center.

Dr. Thomas Sirrio, Director and Chief of Staff at Veterans Medical Center, was delighted beyond belief to have Dr. Hanson and his assistant, Ellen, sign on with his staff. He had been following the models of experimental treatments created by Dr. Hanson and had become a fan of his doctrine and methodology in the treatment of PTSD. He felt very fortunate to have this team in charge of the new wing here. Any major success that Dr. Hanson created in this area of treatment would become a success for him as well.

Ted Hanson's drive to work does feel good this morning, and why not? He's got a lot to feel good about. The warm ride in his Beemer and the relaxing music of Simon and Garfunkel as he drives though the countryside, surrounded by the beauty of it's fallen leaves, was the perfect setting for a pleasant drive to work. He knows he's in a place to call all the shots now and that's the way he's wanted it for a long time. Ted's kind of a rebel in many ways and feels he now has the freedom to pursue a new model of therapy and treatment with fewer bureaucratic restrictions.

Ted was a strong believer in the fact that when you do things in the same old way you get the same old thing. For some reason, the Big Wigs on Capitol Hill never understood that. When it came to the Federal budget cuts for American Veterans' healthcare, the first thing to go, in Ted's mind, was the humor. He was so frustrated with those who raised their right hand and promised one thing and did a left hand deal with the other. Ted did what he had to do until he could do what he wanted. When a newly elected administration in Washington was seated, that time had finally come. Uncle Sam was no longer putting his hands in Ted's shirt and squeezing his tits until they were purple. The problems of wannabe shadow critics and tunnel vision bureaucrats were no longer a boulder in front of his path.

Dr. Hanson is enjoying his ride today, but what he's not aware of is that he and Ellen are on the way to one of the most profound accomplishments of their careers. They will be getting a new patient today, at least one he and Ellen believe to be new. Soon they will discover that I'm not new to them at all. In fact, I was one of the first PTSD casualties of the Vietnam War. They had worked with me at St. Albans back in New York during Dr. Hanson's internship and Ellen had done my initial intake evaluation there. I will be just as surprised to see them and discover that I am assigned to the care of their treatment team as well. The seen is always wrapped in the unseen, and I believe the three of us are going to have an experience with providence that none of us had planned on. Together this trio will become each other's teacher, taught and teaching that will manifest a road of recovery for the treatment of this condition known as Post Traumatic Stress Disorder.

I would have to say that chance has played a more significant role in the direction my life has taken than anything I have ever planned for. Every so often, if we are lucky, we may experience a redemption of the past with a future that is free of fear and guilt. The methodology of Dr. Hanson's treatment model is not about the conquering of an evil. It is about the creation of a therapeutic bridge of coexistence that will allow the crossing and the freeing of an old friend.

2 A.M. Blues

It's 2 a.m., I'm feeling blue. Roused from bed.
Memories of Nam drifting through.

Time again, to put pen to pad. Write of things that make me sad.

Want to let go, put it all to rest. It's enough to know I passed life's test.

Shake with dread from the flooding thoughts.
Put names to faces of those who were lost.

No glory for me or those who served.
Branded "Baby Killers" – of all the nerve.

Relive a time so long ago. Envision a place I had come to know.

Search and DESTROY was the name of the game.
Large body counts brought recognition and fame.

All the battles we fought in places quickly forgotten.
The stench of death so putrid and rotten.

Napalm canisters tumbling through the air.
Instant horror dropped with care.

Vills and hootches burned to the ground. Plenty of pain to go around.

Tag 'em and bag 'em, our brothers in arms.
Their numbers at home brought such an alarm.

They died from our guns, malaria took a few.
Snipers and mines and mortars, too.

So senseless it was the little war we had.
All the people killed - it's enough to make you go mad.

It's 2 a.m., I'm feeling blue. Another sleepless night, nothing new.

used by permission of Lawerence Mize from his book *"Dead Men Calling"*

Chapter 4: Chronic Deja Vu

G ood morning. How's Dr. Ted today?"
"What can I say Ellen? Thank God it's Monday. I couldn't wait to get my butt to work today. With all the unpacking and trying to get things squared away, the weekends for Barb and I have been brutal. When it comes to new furniture and paint colors, Barb and I are at opposite ends of the chart. Her parents are coming over to help out this week. I'm sure that'll swing the vote her way on what's hot and what's not."

Ted and Barb were fortunate in finding a house that suited the needs of their family so close to her parent's home in Towson. There were a lot of young couples raising families in the community and the Hanson's were thrilled with the quality of the public school system. Another bonus was that the school bus stopped right in front of their house. This was a plus for Barb because it freed her up to get more things done at home during the day. Towson was located twelve miles north of Baltimore, with a shopping center and many privately owned variety and specialty shops close by. Everything was within walking distance or a very close drive. Towson was a good place for the Hanson's and they found themselves fitting in very well. What would a town be without a good watering hole and Ted had found one, an Irish pub with live music, folk dancing, good food and cold beer. It was a close getaway place for him and his wife when her parents were available to watch the kids for a few hours.

"How was your weekend Ellen?"
"Fine, Ted, it was just what I needed."
"And, how was that?"
"Restful, thank you."

Ellen rented an old fashioned, but quaint carriage house near the Inner Harbor in Baltimore. Then she went out and found the car of her dreams, a used 1973 Triumph TR-6 British racing green convertible. She loved it and felt the car fit with the character of her small, but charming house. Life was unfolding for her in a new way since her husband's passing and she was finding happiness again in a new place.

"Speaking of need, I've got some coffee ready. Are you up for some?"

"Sure, a cup of coffee and a cigarette sounds good. Thanks, Ellen."

"You know cigarettes are bad for your health. I thought this was your week to quit."

"Yes it was, and perhaps they are, but with as much as I have on my plate right now I find them to be a quick fix for relief."

"So Ted, how's that new Beemer running?"

"Just like your coffee Ellen, strong and smooth."

"Gee, thanks Ted."

"Speaking of smooth, how's our schedule today?"

"Like most Mondays, in a place like this we are busy as hell. You might want to wait and pray for Lent before giving up those cancer sticks."

"Ellen, give it a breather. You don't need to sell it when it's already been sold."

It was common for Ted and Ellen to go back and forth with each other. Their bickering was the wealth of their friendship that took many years to acquire. This was their unbroken circle of trust and just the way they worked.

"Just because you didn't get laid last night is no reason to take it out on me."

Ted laughs and says "Are you ready to start work now?"

"Yes, I suppose I am, otherwise we won't get anything done

today. Grab your coffee and have a seat because I have something to show you. Look at this patient's name and profile with me. He came in over the weekend and we're scheduled to do an intake on him tomorrow."

"OK, that's part of the process. So what's the big deal? Does he walk on fire and water with cool feet or something?"

"Nothing like that but when you're done reading his case history, I'm sure it will have your attention."

"Let me see what we have here..."

"His name is Joe Ross. He was one of our first confirmed psychological casualties of the Vietnam War. He was medically evacuated from Vietnam to St. Albans Naval Hospital in New York on March 24, 1969. He's not a new patient at all, at least not with you and I. In fact, he was under our care when we were interns at St. Albans. Ted, does his name ring a bell with you now?"

"Yes Ellen, it does. Let me think for a moment. Do we have a complete medical history file that may have come in with him?"

"Yeah Ted, we do and I've read it twice so far. Here it is. Can you believe this? Check it out for yourself."

"Oh, my God, I do remember this guy now. Joe Ross was one of the first confirmed cases of Post Traumatic Stress at St. Albans. He was one of my first fieldwork assignments and a fairly young kid as I recall."

"Didn't I say this would get your attention?"

"Yes, you did Ellen, and yes it has."

"What ever happened to him Ted?"

"From what I am reading here, it was the same thing that happened to most of them during those times."

"What was that?"

"They were discharged and released from the military, most of them with nowhere to go except to homeless shelters and the local park benches. Some were happy just to go to jail for awhile - three hots and a cot for free. These guys had nothing and often would sell their blood for five dollars a pint only to spend it at a local liquor store called The Pharmacy Cut Rate, a block from the hospital. People, for the most part, have no idea that many combat veterans walk around feeling a very silent injury deep inside of them. The country never wanted the Vietnam War in the first place, much less the men who came home broken from it. A lot of business owners would refer to them as 'war time help' and refused to hire them. At least the VA isn't putting them on the streets anymore with nothing. Ellen, Joe has experienced this condition longer than any patient we've known. This could be a good thing for us here at Veterans Medical Center. I believe this man is making a last ditch effort at saving himself and somehow we've got to show him that it wasn't a mistake. The history of his condition suggests he would be an excellent candidate for our new Compass of Cognitive Being (COCB) therapy model. I see here in his chart that Joe's been hospitalized on at least five occasions since he was discharged from St. Albans. He has also experienced two suicide attempts, of which he nearly made good on both of them. Well, we have him now and I see this as a second chance that I'm not about to let go of.

From what I am reading in his chart and past medical records, I don't believe anyone will get a third chance with him and I'm not going to let that happen. There are a lot of things moving around deep inside of his subconscious mind and many of them are not nice at all. So let's see what life has taken away from Joe that has brought him back to the hospital and to us."

Doctor Hanson was right. I did have a lot of cruel things floating around inside of my head. PTSD can be like a trick mirror at a carnival. What you are isn't what it reflects back. It's image is often ugly and grossly distorted, leaving you thinking and feeling mentally impaired and physically defective.

"Ted, from what I've read in his record book it's the usual suspects of his disorder."

"Ellen, would you read those symptoms for me as I take some notes here?"

Ellen picked up the file and began to read: "This patient has been diagnosed with acute PTSD, which is a severe and chronic disorder that is permanent in nature. The patient experiences recurrent acute depression with panic attacks, resulting in severe tachycardia. He's experiencing vivid nightmares and is using speed (methamphetamine) to stay awake to avoid having them. He's also experiencing long episodes of suicidal thought and isolation."

I would have to say that Ellen was a one of a kind nurse. When she reviewed a patient's treatment history she did so with the intuitive gaze of a black cat who possessed a sixth sense of clarity, and she knew how to get it right. The moment she began reading my file, the treatment history of my condition jumped right out at her as though it had been written in red instead of black. She could feel that I was in desperate need of somebody to help me.

I can't remember how many night terrors I've experienced, begging Jesus to awaken me from the horror of a dark void that had entrapped me. Often I have awakened abruptly from the arms of a nightmare with my body covered in sweat and my heart beating like it was coming out of my chest. I spent many nights smoking cigarettes and drinking coffee at Dunkin' Donuts, talking with strangers because I was afraid of falling asleep at home alone. I was a regular and as long as I didn't doze off at the counter or fall asleep in a booth, they didn't mind having me around. I used to buy "crossroads" (methamphetamine) from the taxi drivers. I could get 100 crossroads for twenty bucks and they would get me by for a month, easy. During the day I would take 10 milligrams of Valium to relax me enough to fall asleep for five hours or so. The Valium was free because it was prescribed by the Veterans Medical Center. It was never a deep sleep that I ever felt fully rested from. For some reason, I don't recall ever having nightmares during the day - they always occurred at night. I had made two suicide attempts and failed. Inside I was hoping that PTSD would finally claim me and put an end to all of this.

"Ted, I believe his suicide attempts were the only way he could free himself from the suffering of his condition. How has he lived with it all this time? His family felt helpless, not knowing what to do with him, so they just dropped him off at our doorstep here at Veterans Medical Center."

"You know Ellen, that's the way it usually works. The VA had to take him in because of his service connected disability. He has a Priority Rating and that got him here with us. You know what, I think his Priority Rating is what got us there for him. Ellen, what time is our intake session with Joe?"

"It's at 1:00 pm tomorrow after lunch."

"Ellen, is there any way we could do it before tomorrow?"

"No Ted, I don't see how. We're booked today. Remember it's Monday, but Dr. Sirrio will be doing his intake physical exam today and will share that information with us at tomorrow mornings staffing."

"Ellen, I have a feeling in my gut that this may be one of those 'meant to be' kind of things."

"You know, Ted? I feel the same way, too."

"Ellen, there's another thing here I feel is odd."

"What's that Ted?"

"Why would the Chief of Staff here at a major medical center, like Dr. Sirrio, be doing a simple routine intake physical on a new patient?"

"Perhaps he's not a new patient for Dr. Sirrio either "

"Maybe not Ellen. I'm having lunch with him today and I'll bring it up then. You know, this is something I just thought of. Dr. Sirrio is very much aware of our work with COCB therapy. He knows Joe is assigned to our team for evaluation and treatment. I'll bet this just might be his way of monitoring the situation from the get go. Dollface, I'll let you know what's so with this after lunch. Speaking of lunch, it's that time now. Let me call Sirrio to make sure we are still on for noon. Hello, Dr. Sirrio, Ted Hanson. Are we still on for noon today? That's great, I'll meet you in the cafeteria."

Ted always believed in playing fair and working well with others. He preferred that the scales were balanced but if they weren't, as long as they were tilted his way, he didn't give a damn and was happier yet.

"Hey, good afternoon Dr. Sirrio."

"Yeah, same to you Ted. We can forget about the formalities, call me Tom. Have a seat."

"Ok, Tom. When I arrived at the center this morning, I was surprised to hear that a blast from my past had checked in over the weekend. For Ellen and I, this patient goes back a long way. His arrival is a very unexpected surprise and I have a deep interest in working with him again."

"Isn't life funny? Just when you need a fire lit under your ass it shows up from a source you never expected. Let me guess, Joe is on your mind and you are wondering how I ended up doing a routine physical on him. I don't have a big secret here. I saw a memo on my desk atop a new patient file. Normally I would have passed it onto one of the our medical internists. Then I noticed an old blue St. Albans marker on it's cover so I thought 'Hmm…What do we have here?' It appears the three of you have spent time on the same turf before and that's what aroused my curiosity. I read his file and decided I would perform his intake physical personally."

Tom knew that Ted wasn't a wild child who needed his teeth filed, even though he was the new kid on the block. Adventures and wildness are often uncomfortable and Tom simply didn't enjoy those kind of things. He felt Ted was a steady and predictable type of guy, who was enthusiastic and dedicated to the work he and Ellen were performing. Ted was always willing to explore new things with an eagerness that Tom saw as a genuine and heartfelt concern for his patients.

"Tom, how's he doing in that area?"

"I would say he's in poor health now, but I expect him to recover soon if no positives show up in his blood work for Hepatitis C. Mentally I would say he's deep, and I'm not talking about as a conversationalist here. You can relax Ted, a few notes to his chart and a physical exam is where my 'hands on' ends with Joe. He's yours and Ellen's patient and that's the way it will stay, unless the two of you choose otherwise. Look Ted, I'm an advocate of your work here at Veterans Medical Center. I guess that makes me a fan, too, because I know you and Ellen are going someplace with this. My physical on Joe was nothing more than an acknowledgment for me on one of your many record books."

This was just another feather for Ted's cap that let him know the good work that he and Ellen were doing was not going unnoticed.

"Tom, you've done so much for our work here at Veterans Medical Center. Ellen and I just don't know how to begin to show you our gratitude for giving us a thumbs up on our new therapy model of COCB."

"Let's not put the cart before the horse here Ted. We can't forget about Joe. He's the ball we've got to keep our eye on here. If his condition doesn't respond to our jack in the box therapy, then it's worthless and doesn't mean jack shit in plain English. But on the other side of the hand Ted, if this slick thing that you and Ellen have come up with does work, we're there I've got a feeling we'll have a map of this cat we call PTSD. All we have to do then is unfold it and follow the signs that will lead us home with this thing. Many combat veterans live with a tormentor in their head that continuously attacks and punishes them to the center of their soul. It's the cause of untold misery and unhappiness that many veterans live with everyday of their lives. Ted, I've been here for the last twenty years now and I've seen first hand what PTSD has done to good men. We don't have time to fuck around with a twelve step walk in the park here. Your Compass of Cognitive Being, with Joe as it's needle, is going to show us the way to true north and we're going to run with it all the way. Hell, Ted, when it comes down to it I'm an old blood and guts doctor. Give me a man with a bullet hole and there's a good chance I'll pull it out and get him home alive. My work is simple - they don't expect me to think. They just want me to do what needs to be done. On the flip side of the coin, you have a bloodless wound to deal with. Your bullet can't be seen under a microscope. They expect you to know where, when and how it got there in the first place. The only way to get past this is to create or find something that is new and refreshing - a change of direction that works. Ted, yours and Ellen's model of COCB is going to become the net that is going to save a lot of asses around here, including ours. The three of you together are going to tame it, name it, and explain it. Good luck tomorrow with Joe. If there is anything you need just let me know. As far as I'm concerned you have a blank check for what I consider to be a very promising development for the treatment of Post Traumatic Stress Disorder and Acute Anxiety Disorder."

Who's Left To Pray

Who's left to pray for me my Lord?
I've come so far. Can't take no more.

I feel so tired, walked through every door.
Fallen on my knees, prayed from every floor.

I'm still carrying so much guilt and pain.
Tell me Lord do you even know my name?

I've looked for your signs nearly everywhere.
I'm beginning to think Lord...you don't care.

So many died a sinful shame.
Tell me Lord who do I blame?

Vietnam was but a blink of the eye.
You took so many souls. Why Lord? Why?

As I come to approach the end of my life.
The memories still pierce like a sharpened knife.

Who's left to pray for me my Lord?
Will you tell me now before I leave this world?

used by permission of Lawerence Mize from his book *"Dead Men Calling"*

Chapter 5: Coins

A real ball buster for Ted, early on, was the fact that pulling strings in Washington for the needs of disabled veterans and their families was all about contacts and relationships. Contrary to popular belief, getting what you needed from the Senate floor wasn't about shaking hands and kissing babies, it was 'quid pro quo'. Our elected officials preferred ribbon cutting ceremonies that got their pictures in the papers while laying out their best bullshit as headlines that would hopefully suck up to a voting public. Depending on the political climate of the Appropriations Committee, the politicians on Capital Hill could become as two faced as the mask for tragedy and comedy.

The true meaning of red tape in the House was rigid conformity and the bureaucrats in this place were full of it. Most of them were pretty well off because this kind of manipulation often generates a healthy income from the people it preys on, the taxpayers, but it all stays at the top. This rigid conformity takes the life out of a project or plan that could benefit many as a whole. This is what they want because it keeps us dependent upon them. No matter how often the rules of conformity change in a society the face is always the same, like the cover of a Martian cookbook from an old Twilight Zone episode called "To Serve Man".

Ted felt Big Brother conformity did not usually have the best interest in mind for the needs of disabled veterans. Sometimes he had to observe the government guidelines but whenever possible, he would shit can 'em and respond to his deeper instincts in the way he ran his staff and the care he gave his patients.

I've discovered many times that life can be a two sided coin. One side is a lucky bastard and the other is an unlucky son of a bitch. History has a way of repeating itself, especially mine. It's easy to live your whole life after Vietnam forgetting who you are. After a while, Vietnam had a way of taking away everything you thought you were. If you live your life in one place long enough you become that place, and here I was in a Rehab Center again.

One of the things I disliked about any government center was how they always referred to me with my last name first and my social security number second. It was like the Marines all over again with it's name, rank, and serial number thing. Back in the Corps. whenever my last name was called by anyone above the rank of Sergeant I knew some kind of rinky dink bullshit was soon to follow. No matter how many times I end up in a place like this, it always starts with the same old line, "I've got a lot of questions to ask you so this may take awhile." My response was always the same, "Could we start with using my first name from here on out, now that we know my last?" I guess in some ways I cursed my luck for ending up in a place like this again.

There was nothing strange about Vietnam Combat Veterans, but what was strange was the kind of things that we had to deal with. One of those things was waiting for me today at my one o'clock appointment.

During my intake physical yesterday with Dr. Sirrio, I was informed that I would be under the care of Dr. Ted Hanson and his treatment team. I was also informed that he and his assistant, Ellen, had a new therapy for PTSD that just might create some relief for my condition. When I heard this news, let's just say that I wasn't exactly jumping for joy. The last quality time I spent with this doctor was at St. Albans Naval Hospital and as I recall there was no happy ending in it for me. My thought was, if this is the news of the day what can I hope for tomorrow? My life had the security of a floating crap game since I left Vietnam and now this. I just looked up at God and yelled "Don't just look down, help me!"

"Good afternoon Sir, may I help you?"

"Yes, I have a 1:00 p.m. appointment today."

"What's your last name, Sir?"

"It's just Joe."

"Okay. What are the last four digits of your social?"

"3188"

"Thank you. Here you are. Your appointment is with Dr. Hanson. Joe, have a seat in the waiting room and I'll let the doctor know you're here."

"Thank you."

"You're welcome. Dr. Hanson, this is Sally at the desk. Your one o'clock is here."

"Thanks Sally, I'll be right out."

"And Dr. Hanson, there's one more thing."

"What's that?"

"I think he prefers just to be called Joe."

"Thanks for the info, Sally. I'll remember that."

"Hello, Joe?"

A hearty fellow with a kindly look on his face, smiling with crinkles at the corners of his eyes, behind a pair of round wire framed glasses just walked in and greeted me. A soft voice from out of my past that hadn't changed much over the years, has just spoken my name.

"Yeah."

"My name is Ted. Let's go to my office down the hall here."

The last time I saw Ted Hanson he was a Naval Officer at St. Albans Naval Hospital in New York and he was a bit thinner. It looks like he has changed a lot over the years. I can see the days of the starched lab coats and uniforms are now history. That garb's been replaced by some faded jeans, a buttoned down collar shirt and a sport coat. There were a few other changes with Dr. Hanson besides a new wardrobe. He had longer hair now that appeared to be permed and curly with a full beard and a tattoo on his neck that read "Grease". His appearance was perhaps a little out there, and maybe a bit unprofessional for a doctor to be sporting a tattoo such as that on his neck. Ted never believed in going with the flow - rebels seldom do. In his head, the only things that went with the flow were dead fish and shallow concepts. He had a passion for sports cars and motorcycles so I guess that explained the tattoo. To me, he looked like Abbie Hoffman and dressed a lot like James Dean. This should be interesting, I thought, because I didn't know what the hell to make of this guy I was following now. The last time I was asked to walk this way with him I ended up in a homeless shelter on skid row. Perhaps this is why I felt a sense of apprehension about him now. He was the only doctor I worked with at St. Albans and I still had a lot of anger and resentment toward him. I always felt there was something more he could have done to help me, but he didn't.

"You look a lot different now. You don't look like a stiff anymore and I see you ditched that bleached out lab coat."

"Thanks, Joe, I hear that a lot. Have a seat here. Would you like some coffee?"

"Yeah, can I smoke, too?"

"Why not, the coffee's on the table. Help yourself. Hell, it's the middle of the day. I think I'll have some, too. Joe, you and I have done some work together a long time ago. I was an intern at St. Albans Hospital in New York. It was only for a few weeks because you were discharged and released."

"Yeah, Doc, I remember you and that place. The walls were gray and the ceilings a pale white. I remember looking through the windows during the nights at the rain, just staring and thinking about nothing. Everything about that place seemed dark. I recall watching the rats running across the floor at night. I thought about how much better off they were than me. They were happy just being rats with a place to run. So much for the simple things, huh Doc? When I got here over the weekend Dr. Sirrio did my intake physical and evaluation - nice guy. He said I would be under the care of your treatment team and then we chatted about how I felt about it."

"How do you feel about it, Joe?"

"Well, let's just say I would have preferred a different set of circumstances than the ones we have now."

"What circumstances would you prefer?"

"Perhaps me as the doctor and you as the patient."

"What would that change?"

"Then you would know how it feels to be me and what I think about people like you! The last time I saw you was from the other side of a desk at St. Albans. When you discharged me back then it was like you had thrown me to the dogs. Your last words to me were that I needed to find a way to live my life again the best way that I could. I guess I didn't do a very good job of it because here we are together again. People like you can only see what PTSD has done to people like me. You have absolutely no idea of what it's been like living it. Believe me, you don't want to know because it would frighten the hell out of you if you did."

There was an uncomfortable moment that passed between Dr. Hanson and myself as we sat quietly staring at each other. I just couldn't hold back the anger I felt towards this man now for all the pain and loss I had endured for so many years. If there was a worse place then Hell at this moment, I would have suggested that he should consider visiting there.

"And incidentally, thank you for that minute degree of compassion for discharging me back then and leaving me out on the street with nothing and no place to go. Since we're on the subject, let's not forget that I had no meds and absolutely no idea of what was happening to me either. Not much has changed since then. I'm still a stranger in my own life. So, what's new with you besides some stupid looking glasses and a slick Grease tattoo on your neck?"

"Joe, the truth is that you and many others were let down, not only by therapies that didn't work but also by therapists who didn't know. For the most part, other than a few drugs, we had no idea of how to care for this disorder that we now call PTSD. Those were some very dark times for patients and doctors as well. The days of the Thorazine drool and the shuffle that accompanied it are gone, and so are the leather restraints."

"Doc, when I think back to those times at St. Albans, the locked wards and patients slobbering all over themselves, some in chairs and others laying on the floor, it's like a scene in a horror film but it happened to me in real life. It was like having a nightmare about Vietnam and waking up finding myself there. Please tell me that after all these years you have at least come up with something for my condition other than a new label. I didn't come here for the ambience of a rubber room in a government care center. Someplace, somewhere I have a life that's been taken away from me and some goddamned way I've got to get it back again. What I need you to tell me is how in the hell am I going learn to live with this."

"Joe, when it comes to PTSD there are no longer walls between us and what we don't know. There are now only doors that are opening slowly. All in all, therapy is a good thing and although it may ultimately mean healing and hope, it's still going to hurt."

For some reason I had a hunch this guy was past a lot of the traditional abstract B.S. I had experienced with other therapists. I sensed a sincerity in his voice and I felt that I could trust him to help me with this nightmare I was living 24/7.

"Doctor Hanson, after my intake with Dr. Sirrio yesterday he mentioned that you and your assistant have created a new treatment for PTSD. Is that true?"

"Yes Joe, it is and that's why you have been assigned to our treatment team. This therapy model has never been used but the road map we have created from our experience with PTSD has clearly placed us where we've needed to be for a long time."

"Doctor, if I agree to go along with this treatment what's in it for me?"

"Well Joe, let's begin with the truth about PTSD and you. It isn't curable and it is permanent in nature."

"If that's the case, why the hell am I here? If my condition isn't curable then at least tell me how to not live in fear of it."

In the past, my therapy sessions created more questions and concerns with my condition than they ever resolved for my relief and peace as a human being.

"Joe, I said this condition isn't curable. I didn't say it isn't manageable in such a way that would allow you to live a normal life. I've never been a fan of what I call the voodoo therapeutic practice of therapy. Therapists having their patients repeating verbal affirmations of seeing themselves in the light of the divine and resting in the bosom of love when they were really feeling depressed and suicidal was nuts. The practice of psycho-fantasies made me want to howl and sometimes I did when I got fed up."

"Doctor Hanson, what's so different about your therapy?"

"This therapy points to a place within yourself where PTSD and your life can coexist without conflict. This therapy can release you from the struggles and challenges you experience from Post Traumatic Stress Disorder where your life situation can change from disorder back to order once more. This, in turn, will create a space in that head of yours where transformation can take place and become permanent in nature as it was always meant to be."

He came across with a quiet confidence that was well meaning but I had a curiosity that needed an explanation. So I asked him "Why me Doc? What's so different about me?"

"Joe, you have personalized and humanized the PTSD experience longer than anybody we've known. Because of this, you're the best candidate we have to determine the effectiveness of our new therapy model we call COCB (Compass of Cognitive Being). The goal of this therapy for you can be found in two words - peace and harmony. You and this condition of PTSD came together in a very scary place and during a very turbulent time. There's no way to turn that around and go the other way. This condition will always be a part of your life. As a therapist back in the days of therapeutic ignorance, we were in a state of analytical bondage. We believed it was possible to think stuff up that would have all the answers to the dilemmas of the human condition. Once again, the minds of human behavior had it backwards. What we had failed to consider was the fact that this was a problem of the mind, and that being the case, how were we supposed to fix it with the tools of the mind? Doctors and therapists live and work in an imperfect world where our patients expect us to be perfect. Their co-dependency on us occurred because they believed that we knew where we were going. Joe, what we as doctors have to remind ourselves here is simply this. Angels and demons, just as well as heaven and hell, all come from the same place. They all occupy the same penthouse of our home place located at the very top level of our own heads. We pay a premium price to live there and that price is the fear of being evicted from the only place we've ever known. Sometimes the devil we know is better than the devil we don't know. COCB therapy isn't about saving a person from their demons within. It's about learning how to live with them because they don't take vacations and they're grandfathered in for the long term."

"Dr. Hanson, I have to admit your therapy is very different from anything I'm used to and because of that, I'm not sure if I'm ready to place my faith in you with a therapy that has never been tried before. Not to mention, I've never met a doctor with funky hair like yours and a weird tattoo on his neck. You and this therapy both seem a little out there to me."

"Joe, you've heard of Albert Einstein, haven't you?"

"Yeah, everybody knows about Albert Einstein."

"Einstein had funky hair and very weird expressions. Many of his colleagues viewed him, to say the least, as being a bit on the far side. Albert Einstein was quite possibly the most intelligent person who ever lived. His theories and ideas were so far ahead of his time that, even now, the smartest scientists alive are still discovering his value. What his colleagues saw as just a black board on a wall, he envisioned as a black hole of the universe waiting to be explored. The fingers of his hand held a simple piece of chalk that could someday expose the secrets of space.

Some of the most renowned physicists of today suggest his insights may have been the result of a phenomenon known as automatic writing. Sigmund Freud was a practitioner of automatic writing and he felt it was a tool that could be instrumental in the research and study of human psychoanalysis. Freud considered automatic writing as a means that transcended the rules of logic and directly communicated with the depth of the subconscious mind. Einstein saw the black board as a portal that could transcend time and space."

"Dr. Hanson, how long do think I'll be in therapy with this new progam?"

"Joe, I know in some ways we're writing the rules here as we go but I can tell you this, COCB therapy is not about reaching out in hope of finding a quick fix. There isn't any. Often things must be terribly hurt before they can begin to heal. It's about relearning and using what is already within each one of us. My success as a therapist will be when a patient can place more confidence in the practice of therapy awareness to provide him peace, than taking a pill to hide his pain. Joe, there's one more thing I am hoping for in all this."

"What's that Doctor Hanson?"

"To be fired at the end of therapy by my patient."

"Why?"

"I hope for a job well done, and that I am no longer needed."

"Doctor Hanson, how will I know when I've made peace with these demons?"

"When you have discovered that you can call them friends and no longer have to ask that question anymore."

One of my most defining moments as a human being happened when I realized most of my yesterdays were screwed. On the upswing, I didn't have to deal with them anymore. The good thing here is that all of my tomorrows were full of the possibilities of whatever I wanted.

Everybody is looking for an angle to play and I sensed freedom with this one so I surrendered and started over again. As far as I was concerned, this therapy could be the magic wand I had hoped for. It might be something I could use forever to bring change to my life that seemed entirely appropriate and right for me. I also liked the fact that good work with therapy could mean transcending hell and finding peace and happiness once more.

The years that followed my therapy with Doctor Hanson were very much a 'two steps forward and one step back' kind of thing, which was shorthand for the sessions of relearning how to focus my will, self control, creativity, and using my energy wisely. In many ways Doctor Hanson and I were just two very unusual people who had found a connection and I may have been the phoenix that he was determined to see arise again from it's ashes.

No one is an island.

We were created to explore the seas.

A warm sunny place with a blue sky

and a gentle breeze

are an invitation for us from the universe

to experience the healing waters of life

again and again.

Chapter 6: The Rehab Grad

March 3, 1988
Veterans Hospital PTSR Wing
Baltimore, Maryland
13 Years Later

H ey, Joe   You're here to see Dr. Hanson I take it."
That's right Sal, I'll just have a seat here while you hook me up
with the Doc."

This area of the treatment center was designated as the Post
Traumatic Stress Recovery Unit. It was responsible for the medication
and therapy needs of veterans - mostly Nam Vets that were diagnosed
with PTSD. Across the hall was another unit known as the PPH
(Partial Psychiatric Hospital). This facility was for the needs of PTSD
patients who required the daily care of an ongoing recovery unit but
were not in need of being admitted as full time patients requiring the
care and supervision of around the clock hospital care. These patients
were here for eight hours a day, five days a week. They were allowed
home for nights and weekends if their physical and mental health
conditions permitted it.   The PPH program was a thirty day
commitment and for most Vets one tour in this unit was enough. My
condition was chronic and, as usual, my history had a way of
repeating itself. I had required the needs of this unit twice.

Sometimes the scars and sadness of a hidden war can run deeper
for some than others.

Dr. Hanson was the clinical head of both of these departments and he worked closely with his support staff of mental health therapists and clinical social workers to provide and maintain the highest quality of care possible.

Today was just another day and it was business as usual here at the center. The phones were ringing, an appointment here and a cancellation there. Patients were signing in and signing out. Everything was moving here and Sally, the receptionist, made sure that it moved smoothly for all concerned. She was beyond charming in casual conversation but she also believed that there was such a thing as a stupid question, especially from interns that were fresh out of Med School and new on the job. Sally wasn't somebody to be pressed by an issue that she felt was nonsense. She could shoot you with a look that suggested you give that bone to another dog, and now! She had no patience for know-it-alls, and those who were, found their schedules so crammed they would be working seven days a week for the duration of their residency here.

"I hear today's your last session with Doctor Hanson. We're going to miss seeing your face around here."

"Thanks Sally, that was nice of you to say. I'm going to miss you guys, too."

This day had finally come and I was at the end of a journey that had begun so many years ago. I didn't feel like I was wearing a sign on my back anymore that read "Hexed". With some folks it was all about where you are from. For me, it was all about where I was going. It was time to take my place in the world and this was the first step of a new journey.

"Joe, of all things, is it true that you're going to Minnesota to learn about hair, as in becoming a hairdresser?"

"That's true Sally. The news sure does get around fast."

"That kind of news does. There's not too much of that kind of buzz in a place like this very often. Minnesota is a long way to go and a cold place to be rolling up hair."

"Yeah Sally it is but when I consider where I've been and how far I've come, that school up north just doesn't seem that far away. It's the finest school in the country for what I want to do and besides, I'm ready for a change of scenery. I have an opportunity to class up my life some so I'm going to take it. I'm thinking a beauty school would be a great place to start."

"A guy like you at a beauty school, talk about a kid in a candy store."

"Don't worry Sally. You'll always be my first love. I could never find a mother figure to replace you."

"Thanks. You really know how to wow a girl. Drop us a line to let us know how you are doing."

"I'll do that for sure, Sal. You don't have to worry about me, I'll be fine."

"Not so fast Buster! There's something else I'm going to miss about you."

"Oh yeah, what's that?"

"It's your boy-like, smart ass charm. I've always been a sucker for it."

"Thanks Sally. For a moment I thought you were going to make sport of me before I left. What can I say? One has to own up to the truth. I do what works for me and my angle is my smart ass charm. It's my language of the deal and it always leaves me with the last word."

"Oh, you're a clever one. I never would have guessed. Good luck Joe, and like I said, write!"

"Is that Joe out there flirting with my receptionist again?"

"That would be me Doc, but I think we're practicing verbal Judo more so than flirting."

"Come on back here and have a seat my friend. The meter's running."

"How're you doing today, Doc?"

"I'm doing just fine. The question is 'How are you doing?' You're going to be a hop, skip and a jump away from here soon so let's talk some about your future."

"We've worked together a long time to get here Doc but now I feel an emptiness, like I'm leaving something behind and I can't figure out what it is. I've made a great achievement and yet, I feel a sadness and a sense of loss."

"That emptiness you feel is normal. It means you've let go of the past and now you're ready to step out into the future. It's time to turn the page of that book and begin a new chapter in your life. The fact that you're moving on is the direction our therapy has always been focused toward. It's good to try new things that we're not sure we can do. Sometimes we're amazed at what we can pull off. Remember way back at the beginning I told you my goal as a therapist was to be fired by you someday for a job well done. We've reached that time now and I think that both of us know that I am no longer needed."

"Doc, I guess I've had enough time to figure what I want and I feel that Minnesota is the right place for me but there's some uncertainty in my head wondering if I am doing the right thing."

"What do you see out there to fear?"

"Nothing."

"That's right. Joe, in therapy we talked about how you can feel about something one way and think about it in another. Whenever you find yourself in this situation, always go with your gut. Not long ago people thought of emotions as old stuff, as just feelings - feelings that had little to do with rational decision making or got in the way of it. Now that position has reversed. Intense focus can make a difference. Gut feelings about threats or opportunities can be correct. Your thoughts can be pathological liars but your feelings are the messengers of truth. Your mind is going through an anxiety experience of not knowing what is next for it now. It's generating doubt and confusion that it uses as a self defense mechanism of protecting what it knows. You are going on an adventure into the unknown, and that's a good thing because you're ready for it. The focus of meaningful therapy is learning to live with the aspect of uncertainty. It sucks sometimes, but it lets you know you can handle whatever happens to you. Mentally making a decision and physically acting on it, instead of wishing and hoping that things will fall into place for us, is more realistic than trying to create a make believe world which never produces true security. The truth is, there's a new emptiness inside of you and you no longer have the weight of your emotional fears on your back anymore. That boulder is gone and now there's a space for something new to take root and grow. The good news is, I believe it will happen sooner than you think. Sometimes fate gets off on itself as being invincible. I guess that depends on how we choose to see it, as divine intervention or Murphy's Law. You've always had a strength of character within yourself. Our therapy was just a means to rediscover it."

"Doc, what helped me so much was that you talked more than any shrink I've known."

"Joe, I speak the stuff - I didn't say I knew how to do it. That's why we do therapy so we can practice for that place we call next time. Just think of therapy as a mind and identity enhancement exercise... no pain, no gain. Therapy can be like a social lubricant. It helps people to open up. It has served its purpose and now you're ready to fly again. Let's chat about this school in Minnesota you are going to. I feel it's a good thing, and perhaps you've found your niche. It sounds like you've taken the practical action that may have bought you the ticket for a new life."

"Thanks Doc. I feel that way about it, too."

"So, when did you come up with the idea of working with hair?"

"It's not a new idea, Doc. It's been in my head for years and I finally decided to do it. When I was a kid in Baltimore I swept the floor and took out the trash at Tony's Barber Shop. Tony was good to me and so were the customers. Somebody always wanted a sandwich from the deli or a pack of cigarettes. I was a 'go for' and didn't mind keeping Tony's customers happy and besides, there was always a tip in it for me. Tony kept an eye on me and made sure my young ass stayed out of trouble and I had something my pals didn't."

"What was that?"

"A job with spending money. Maybe it was Tony's generosity and kindness that gave me the idea to do hair."

"What's the name of that school in Minnesota?"

"It's called the Horst Institute for Hair."

"Is the school V.A. approved to attend?"

"Yes Doctor Hanson. They accept veterans and the GI Bill. All the paperwork is done."

"When do you start school?"

"Next week, but I'm leaving on a train tonight. My sister, Jean, is giving me a ride to the station. I'm packed and ready to go."

"Do you have a place to stay up there?"

"Yes I do, and what a streak of luck I ran into. My sister has a friend who owns a large house on Fraternity Row in a place called Dinkytown in Minneapolis. It turns out the Fraternity lost it's charter and is no longer a Frat House, but they still need to pay the lease. I made a call and spoke to a guy by the name of Randy, who runs things there. He said as long as I was a student and paid the rent he didn't care what school I went to."

"What Frat was that Joe?"

"It was a Jewish Frat House and the cool thing about it is it's walking distance to my school."

"I don't think I have to worry about you - it all sounds good.

An ex-Marine, a Nam Vet at that, who's a straight guy going to a beauty school while living in a Jewish Fraternity House that has lost it's charter. Joe, your world has taken a new turn."

"Thanks Doc. You know what else is on my mind?"

"What's that?"

"I wish Ellen could have been here now. It's too bad we lost her a while back. She put in a lot of time working with me and I miss her a great deal. No matter how much pain she suffered from her cancer, she still worked hard to give guys like me a second chance at life when there wasn't one left for her."

"Joe, is there something you would like to say to Ellen if she were here now?"

"Yeah Doc, there is."

"Why don't you just go ahead and say it."

"Ellen, thank you for being with me while I was going through all those battles when I needed you the most. We all need someone or something that can help us to heal our wounds, and thank you for being there for me. Someone someplace in heaven must have needed you to purify the wounds from a spear he suffered while upon a cross and you were kind enough to grant him a house call."

"Joe, those were very wonderful and heartfelt words you just said. Bad times have a way of waking us up to the good things we're not paying enough attention to. Just remember to always do what is in your heart and you will be fine. "

"I guess visiting hours are over. I've got to go now. Let's just say goodbye and you take care of yourself. I'll never forget you, Doctor Hanson."

"Congratulations Joe! Our time is up now. That's it. You're done. You're a free man. I hope we can keep in touch."

"What time is it?"

"It's six thirty Joe."

"That's funny."

"Why, are you running late?"

"No. It's because I had a broken watch in Vietnam that stopped at six thirty and I felt like it told me twice a day that I was still alive. Now that time is telling me to get going and start living again."

"A school can be a great place for direction. I guess it's time to put my money on the table and Joe, I'm betting on you to win. Goodbye my friend."

"So long Doc."

I was never able to believe in myself until I met Dr. Hanson, who showed me how much he believed in me over the years nor did I know how much I could receive until I discovered how much I was able to return. Now it was time to face up and meet myself head on.

"Dr. Hanson, it's Sally."

"Yes Sally, what is it?"

"We have a new patient from the Naval Hospital in Bethesda. His chart just arrived today and he'll be here tomorrow. Should I schedule an intake evaluation exam?"

"What's the nature of his condition?"

"He's a Marine who was just medically evacuated from Lebanon for acute PTSD."

"By all means Sally. I want to see him as soon as possible."

We can honor our spirits as human beings
by listening to the rhythmic beats

of life and love that are always
within our own hearts.

To be aware, to act, to sense and to be silent.

We are the fabric of life that was created
out of the stars and the air.

There have been times in my life when I felt
I was between someplace and nowhere.

When I found myself alone,

I knew not to worry that providence
would soon arrive and find that I was here.

Chapter 7: The House

I waved so long to Baltimore last night as I boarded a train bound for Minneapolis. I was fresh out of a Veterans Medical Center and on my way to begin my new life as a student. I slept most of the night during the trip, which helped me to conserve money that I didn't have to spare for expensive meals on the train. Money was tight now and it was going to require some clever juggling of my resources until I could find a way to produce an income other than my school grant from the Veterans Administration to live on.

Uncle Sam was footing the bill for my tuition at the Horst Institute for Hair. As a Disabled Veteran, I was sitting on a winning lottery ticket so I decided to cash in on it. It was an all expense paid trip for one but the rub was that it could take up to six weeks before I got my first check. I didn't care because I was riding on Uncle Sam's dime and his credit was always good, even if mine wasn't.

When I arrived in Minneapolis, my first order of business was to report to the Whipple Building at Fort Snelling and meet with my Vocational Rehab Counselor, Mr. Erickson. I could tell this guy was going to be a prick the moment I met him. The light in my head went off when he came across more like a Probation Officer than a Rehab Counselor, with his brash tone and abrupt manner. I felt like he was ignorant to the fact that I was a patient that had been discharged from a hospital and not a prisoner who had been released from a detention center. His job was to supervise my attendance and progress during my enrollment at the Institute and to make sure that my financial needs as a student were met. He was the "cash cow" that stood between the government and me that covered my ass. This guy was going to track everything I did as a student and if I wasn't in school on any given day, he made it clear that I would be getting a phone call that demanded an explanation of why I was absent. Considering I was a Nam Vet who had just gotten out of a mental hospital and would soon be attending a beauty school, I didn't need much of this kind of help to be completely screwed. I knew I was on sacred ground as long as I never challenged or crossed this guy in any way, shape or form. What can I say, maybe I was living a charmed life and didn't know it.

It's March in Minnesota and the city of Minneapolis sits under an Arctic sun floating in a cobalt sky that's as cold as blue blazes. It has a misleading appeal that's often inviting but can quickly become a wind chilling experience. I have to say, Minnesota nice can be very welcoming but southern hospitality has a true sense of warmth. I've come to know that God is truly timeless and has been timely many times in my life, when I least expected it. Often I felt he was unpredictable, narcissistic, and weird when it came to his plans regarding me.

I have been here for three days now and I've rented a room in a Jewish Fraternity House which recently lost it's charter. It wasn't for allowing a Catholic Irish boy like me to move in but it was because all the original chartered members had graduated and moved out, except for one. The remaining student body of the house could no longer meet the requirements for membership of the brotherhood set by the Jewish Fraternal Order and Governing Council so it's charter was revoked.

So why did they let me in? Here's the long and short of the skinny. The house may have lost it's charter as a Frat but it was still on the hook for the lease. The one and only remaining chartered member of the Fraternity was a smart guy by the name of Randy, now acting as the House Manager, who came up with a super idea that just might save the remaining beanie babies of the house of David. Randy was now the Ways and Means Committee for any creative ideas to increase funds that were needed to maintain the house as a student living facility on Fraternity Row. What he was about to suggest could be considered ironic for a Jewish Frat House, but just as ironic was a Jewish household that was financially embarrassed.

Randy scheduled a house meeting and presented a plan for consideration by the student body. He expressed in a humorous manner that this would be an excellent time to contribute support for the alliance of Christians and Jews. Randy shared his ideas for renting a couple of rooms to non-Jewish students as a financial means of making ends meet. Now that the house was no longer a habitat strictly for Jewish culture, he felt it would be discriminatory and nonproductive not to rent to Gentile students. Randy was going to have a tough sell today on the budget floor of the house to even consider a cohabitation. The collective consciousness of his audience was that there were many charismatic primates in the world but the ones that are fascinating in the concrete jungle might not make for good domestic partners. Perhaps, some things were better off left in their own habitat.

Randy was now a one man campaign for change. "We'll give them an olive branch and the Shagits will in turn pay us the gelt we need to keep our Kibbutz from sinking into the Dead Sea," Randy joked. "Brothers, look at it this way. I'm not asking for a pound of flesh here. It's time to refocus, reform and renew our priorities."

Randy must have been very persuasive. After a lot of hoopla the stones were cast, the votes were in, and it was a done deal. When the meeting was over everyone stood up, threw their beanies in the air, yelled "Mazeltov" and made like a bat out of hell for Spring Break. What Randy didn't share during the meeting was his plan to rent out the entire first floor from time to time to other Frats for their kegger parties. This would bring in some additional cash flow for the house and if the parties were ever busted by the cops, the active Fraternities would not be held responsible for the consequences of any legal issues nor the reprimands and possible expulsion from the University. Randy was creating a modern day speakeasy right here on campus with the finest location possible, the first house on Fraternity Row. Randy's plans had appeal and the potential for some damn good cash to be made under the radar. He only needed one thing to pull it off, a silent partner, an outsider, somebody whom he could trust and rely on who wasn't part of the existing inner circle. An opportunist so to speak, but who?

Little did he know that an Irish Catholic Mick from the East Coast, recently released from a mental hospital, would soon arrive and be the answer to his prayers. Soon I would be granted entrance and allowed cohabitation with the chosen people. It didn't matter what school I was attending. The fact that I was a student, even at a beauty school, granted me squatting rights in the soon to be reformed house of David.

Another plus for renting a room to a non-Jewish student was the possibility that he or she would be willing to perform general housecleaning services on an ongoing basis for a significant reduction in rent. Randy saw this as twice the thrill for half the bill.

I called Randy from the train station when I arrived and he was kind enough to pick me up, take me to the V.A. for my paperwork regarding school, and bring me to the house. Randy had good reasons for being happy the day I showed up. He was the man with the plan and I was going to become a part of it.

For the most part, the place was empty because of Spring Break. The lost tribe would be returning sometime this weekend to attend classes beginning Monday, including me. The Horst Institute had scheduled an orientation on Monday for new students with classes beginning on Tuesday.

There are so many unknowns here for the time being. I've never lived around a Jewish neighborhood, much less in a Jewish household. I considered it a blessing that I was lucky enough to rent the only room available at this time for a non-Jewish student. Randy could have waited it out for a Jewish home boy to show up, but he didn't. He appears to be a sensitive fellow and I think he may have felt the urgency of my need for housing since school was starting on Monday.

Randy said "Let's take a tour of the house. I'll show you the room and let's see what you think." The house was messy on the inside, which wasn't unusual when you consider it's youthful tenants, but my room looked like the junk room of a skid row hotel that was full of the shit that nobody wanted. When I first saw it I felt like I was presented with a task that somebody else had failed at. What I thought of as 'sloppy seconds' would turn out to be the lucky break that I needed. The last roomie left a sign with a smiley face which read "Karma is a Bitch". There was trash, beer and pop cans all over the place, and let's not forget about the cigarette butts that covered most of the floor. The last ass who hibernated here was booted out and left the room a mess as if to say "Fuck You" to the House Manager. I didn't like the room at all but I kept my thoughts to myself.

I said "This place is fine and it's close to school. I'll take it."

With school starting Monday and being in a place I didn't know jack shit about, this was no time to be picky. Having no place to go and only five hundred bucks in my pocket it was time for a spit in the hand and a shake on a deal. I asked Randy "How much for the room?" He said the house normally charged three hundred dollars a month but if I was willing to do some house cleaning on a weekly basis he would cut that in half. The room looked like hell but Randy made it a gift from heaven. I signed on and paid up, which now gave me a foot hold on the West Bank area of the University.

Randy seemed as happy about the deal as I was and showed me where the cleaning supplies were kept with the mops, brooms and vacuums. He then gave me two keys, one for my room and another for the supply closet. Randy said it would be a good thing having me do the house cleaning and it would definitely add to the creature comforts of living in the house. He gave me a pat on the back and said "I'll see you later this week and incidentally, if possible have the house cleaned by the end of Spring Break." I said "No problem. Thanks again." Randy may have been testing me to see how well I could do the job at hand before, perhaps, offering me some more lucrative work in the future.

After he left I sat on the floor in the middle of my room looking at all the disarray that surrounded me and I thought "How in the hell am I going to handle this?" My temperament wasn't suited for this much of a clean-up job. I've rented a room in a house, at a place, for a life that I wasn't sure how to live. I didn't know what to make of this place. Right now it just looked like a bad scene. I was just going to have to take it one day at a time until I could see how things were going to pan out. All I could think to myself was that action was related to success just as hesitation was to failure and I'd best get off my ass now and start acting on the behalf of my success.

In so many ways, life has teased me with the humor of its charm when I felt it was anything but charming. I knew I had lucked out finding a room so close to the Institute that I could afford. This was a big break for me and I felt very appreciative for this kind act of providence. I had to keep in mind that if something is meant to be it tends to happen quickly and I knew I had to respond just as quickly or it would become a lost opportunity. I just felt so overwhelmed by a room which appeared more like a landfill needing a backhoe instead of a room to comfort a student in a Frat Shack.

I had found the place that I needed for the things I had come here to do. Moving to Minneapolis helped me to think and feel better about the world and the people in it. In many ways, the Frat Shack was going to serve as my transitional housing that would gradually allow me to comfortably reenter society again. For the last thirteen years I had been in and out of more hospitals and treatment centers than I could remember. I had been institutionalized and I knew I didn't want to die that way. As a patient, I had no responsibilities other than to do what I was told and when to do it. One day I just told myself "Enough is enough. I deserve a better life than this" and I made up my mind that I was going to do whatever it took to get my head back together again. When you're a patient in a mental hospital you have very little to be accountable for. Responsibility and accountability for yourself returns after the healing has begun. Sooner or later the confidence returns and when it does, you're out the door and on your own again.

Well here I am, and can you believe it starts with me cleaning up the left behind shit of somebody else's screwed up life? We all start at the beginning with somebody else wiping our ass for us and I guess my time had come to return the favor.

I may have looked like a flower in a swamp but I had a heartfelt feeling of success. I had created a new beginning in an unknown place, out of an unheard of situation. It had taken so much determination to get to this point and failure was not an option.

Drastic times call for drastic measures and my skills of multitasking came to the rescue so I got up and did what needed to be done. If cleanliness was next to godliness, this place was hell and meant for it's keepers. I wore a germ mask and rubber gloves to protect my health from the unknown biohazards in the performance of my duty. I started with my room and then the rest of the house, cleaning all four floors including the windows, bathrooms and those damn sliding doors. This act of working like a kitchen bitch from hell took about two and a half days. I was cursing like a sailor until the house finally started to look like it had the gloss of a spit shine. These bathrooms could now pass any Drill Instructor's inspection who had a hard on for a white glove test.

I enjoyed giving credit where credit was due, especially when it was due for me. Privately, I stood back and admired the results of my handiwork and even gave myself a pat on the back for a job well done. Maybe others would notice and follow suit. It was a lot of work to take on and when I started, I did everything I could to make sure the end result was going to be worthwhile. I wanted Randy to know he could count on me to keep my end of our bargain.

After completing the clean up job from hell for the house of the Holy, my timing could not have been better. Right about then the veterans of the Muscle Beach landing were returning home from Spring Break to the concrete driveways of Fraternity Row. With them came the stories of conquest and the high fiving acknowledgments of each other's kiss and tell bragging rites of passage, proudly showing off the sunburns, knee burns, and rug burns often encountered while advancing on new physical terrain. I just stood there eyeballing the area while taking all of this in. These guys reminded me of an earlier time in my life with their bravado and invincible attitude. Considering my age, it felt like a lifetime ago. Then Randy came walking through the door. There were lots of shouts, cheers, and high fives. The lost tribe had returned and the boys were back in town. Randy looked around and then straight at me, he gave me a nod with a smile that said "The house looks good. I like it."

There was an advantage to being the new guy on the scene, especially in a new place. I definitely caused a stir and those around me immediately wanted to know who I was. I felt like a grown-up adult, knowing that I was an original test tube baby, and somebody was going to try convincing others that we were all created equal when I knew better. Their curiosity of who the hell I was and why I was here was about to end. For some reason, I had the feeling that a radical introduction was about to take place. Randy took a deep breath and crossed his fingers behind his back as he spoke the sweet words of a man of my own heart. "Everybody quiet! A moment please. This is my cousin Joe. He's from Baltimore, no I mean Boston. He is out of the Marines and a new student at the Horst Institute. I am also very happy to say my cousin will be living here in the house with us while he is attending school in Minneapolis." A moment of silent contemplation followed this spoken enigma of family ties that

Randy had presented. There is a way to have your cake and eat it, too. It just requires that you get very creative, and perhaps a bit sneaky. Most of the soon to be doctors, lawyers and dentists of this now fallen house of Israel had known one of Randy's parents was a convert to Judaism by marriage so having a Catholic cousin from the East Coast wasn't too much of a stretch. I was considered family and I was in!

"Joe, why would you want to live here? Never mind that for now, tell us after the party."

"What party?"

"The kegger we are throwing here tonight at the house."

For an Irish Mick like me, having a free keg of cold beer with plenty of food and music to go around and nobody had died yet was reason enough for a celebration in itself. This place was starting to feel like home with the boys already and I hadn't even gotten drunk and fought with them yet! The diversity of this group was going to contribute to an active and interesting night.

Jeff and Tommy showed up with a keg and a dozen pizzas were soon on their way. The stereo was pumping out the sounds of Bob Marley and a slight fog of weed smoke was in the air. The house and the people who lived here, and that included me now, had a wonderful way of affecting my life in a way that I hadn't expected. As I looked around at the blushed faces, big smiles and shiny eyes under the waves of some of the best music I had ever heard before, I could see the perks and privileges of some fantastic situations coming into my life. I could see myself becoming a party animal and dating a lot of younger women. What most guys my age were wishing for I was going to be living. There I stood with a cup of beer in one hand and a Marlboro Red in the other while having the time of my life and I was thinking "Holy shit! I get to do this for the next two years". I was here with all these cool people and Randy was introducing me to someone new every few minutes.

"This is my cousin Joe. He's a student at the Horst Institute and living here in the house."

"Hey, Joe, is Randy kidding? You're really a student and living here in the Frat Shack?"

"Sure am."

"How long will you be at Horst?"

"Decades, I hope."

"So, do you think you can handle this crowd?"

"You know it! You guys are crazy and messy, but I love crazy and messy."

We were on Fraternity Row and this party was going to last all night. Students walking by the house saw the action, just came in and joined us. We didn't care and no way in hell were any of us going to ask these ladies to leave. We weren't that stupid or cheap with the beer.

I was having a great time and believe me, I gobbled it up. I couldn't remember when I had as much of a good time as I was having tonight. In a short time my life had turned another corner. I was no longer the FNG (fucking new guy), but just another face in the crowd that lived in the house and went to a school. I loved it, enjoyed it and I had a blast! We may not have been of one family but we sure as hell were of one house.

Welcome To The Horst Institute

You are here because your mothers

could not teach you

how to become hairdressers.

This school is not for everyone,

but

it might be for you.

We'll see.

Chapter 8: School Circle

March 8, 1988

D amn, just let me sleep another five minutes please? It's the bells from hell again. My alarm clock is screaming–Time to get up, now! Okay, you win. I'll do it, but first a cigarette. Where the hell are they? I can't see shit in the dark. "Turn a light on dummy," says an awake thought in my head. Here they are on the floor next to the bed where I left them. After I smoke this butt, I'll do the shower thing to clear my head and get things together. My first school morning wake-up here in the Frat Shack felt like the first run of a half-ass morning show that was going to last all day. The show was on but when it came to the script, I didn't have a clue. With the kegger over the weekend, a hangover that followed and my clean up crew of one, my butt was dragging. Let's peek out the window and see what we've got. Looks like it's still dark and cold outside. At 5:30 a.m., I guess it is. The snow is blowing in the air and on the streets. It's one hell of a day to begin great plans and big things.

I'm not used to getting up so early in the morning but with school starting today I'd best make it a new habit. It's so quiet here in the house with the exception of my two-bell, jack-hammer alarm clock that's anal about performing on time. I needed an alarm clock for school so I picked one up cheap from a secondhand store. Now I know why it ended up there. It must have been donated for the hearing impaired. That store should have paid me for taking it off their hands.

The rooms in the Frat Shack will be lighting up soon. We are all due back at school today. The beanie babies will be at the U of M doing what beanie babies do - learning that doctor and lawyer stuff. As for me, well, I'm going to a beauty school. The Horst Institute and I will be the teacher and the taught for the next two years. Thank God it's quiet because this thought is still being processed. I'm excited about living in the Frat Shack and going to a beauty school but this early in the morning everything is a work in progress, including me at the moment.

I can hear lots of cars and buses on University Avenue as they go by the house on the way to the U of M. The morning rush hour is taking place right outside of my bedroom window. Waking up to the sounds of diesel engines and car horns is going to take some getting used to. The steady sounds of traffic outside of my window complimented the steady flow of thoughts inside of my head. It seems like my mind and the outside world are both going a lot of places at once today.

I'll be walking eight blocks of the Arctic Circle via Dinkytown to the Institute - a fast walk, you betcha! I've only been here a week and I'm already speaking Minnesotan. Who knows? Maybe my daily walk, or perhaps I should say my run, to and from school in this small part of the Ice Cap will become a character building experience for me. I sure as hell hope so because with the environmental conditions being as they are, I'm going to need something to replace the abandonment of my physical warmth.

It's time to split. School starts in about an hour and I need a cup of coffee and some toast along the way. The sun is out and the sky is a beautiful blue without a single cloud. I thought things were looking up but when I stepped out the door - holy mother f *%#!@, God was it cold!

Folks here wear a thing that covers their entire head with the exception of holes for their eyes, nose and mouth. Now I know why - they're not robbers or terrorists, they're cold! I've got to get me one of those things and soon.

It was a short walk to school, but it's so damn cold out here that it wasn't long before my face was numb, my ears were stinging and the tip of my nose felt frozen. Wow! Jim's Café across the street from school, that works for me. I only hope it's not a mirage. I've got fifteen minutes to spare, just enough time to down breakfast and grab a pack of cigarettes.

It feels good to be out of the cold for a short break. This place must be popular with the student body of the Institute because it's full of them and, perhaps, a few instructors as well. There's a lot of action going on here for a small café on a cold street corner so early in the morning. It's like the morning social hour here before school. Jim's Café was full of cigarette smoke, waitresses yelling breakfast orders, jukebox music, and maybe a hundred conversations of anything you could imagine all taking place at the same time. Looks like a lot of foot traffic across the street and I think I had better join the herd now. It seems like everybody else here has the same idea because this place is starting to empty out fast. "This is it," I thought, "These are the first steps of a second chance that I had worked so hard for" as I made my way across a cold street and entered the Institute.

This is the first time I have walked through the doors of this school and I think it has just blown my mind. I can't believe what I am seeing here. I've never seen a place like this before and the experience is kind of refreshing in a manner that I am not sure how to describe. The path of my recovery has run through a lot of places but I've never seen one as striking in it's appearance and as peaceful with it's presence as this one. The beauty of this place is beyond words. This was a real head trip that I could definitely get into without dropping a pill. The smell of exotic scents was in the air and the soft, almost hypnotic, music of Enya was in the background. I had to stop and take it all in for a moment. I immediately felt a connection here. It was wild, the people were cool, and I liked it a lot. The meter was running and I was definitely going along for this ride. I was at a place where I was supposed to be and it was here.

It was easy to see that this school was about art, beauty and life. These were the things that would change how I saw myself and the world. The students here dress and look so different than the ones I live with at the house who are attending the U of M. Lots of cool looking hair and polished European style to go around with a common display of attitude that was proudly expressed like a fashionable accessory.

Not knowing exactly where I was going, I asked an instructor for directions to my class. She was kind enough to escort me to the lower level of the building and right to my classroom door. "Sarah, I believe this one belongs to you."

"Good Morning!" Sarah said as she greeted me with a smile. "Welcome to the Horst Institute. What is your name?"

"My name is Joe Ross."

"Here is your name tag and your student ID number is 129. I'll give you a time card later today. My name is Sarah. Find a desk where you like and have a seat. We'll be starting in about five minutes or so."

Here I am sitting in a classroom with about twenty students or so. It's our first day and nobody knows each other well enough to be gabby yet. That will change by lunch time and so will the pecking order of who's who in the class.

A few small talk conversations are taking place but most of us are waiting in quiet anticipation of how things are going to unfold once the day begins. I am casually eyeballing the area while checking out the new creative talents in the room. Hell, I'm old enough to be anyone's father here, except for some of the instructors. What a thought - Maybe that'll count for something like respect for your elders. I just felt a smile on my face - Father figure, I hope not! I'm not that kind of material, at least not for now. With my spiked hair, attitude and tattoos, I'm pretty sure my mission statement easily reads 'Rebel, with a lot of causes'!

Speaking of a mission statement, I think one just marched into the room all dressed in black and he sure as hell doesn't look like Johnny Cash to me. His uniform of the day was a black beret over his blond hair, a black sweatshirt, and black Docker pants finished off with a pair of black Doc Marten boots. He looked more like a Storm Trooper at a reeducation camp than an instructor at a beauty school. When he introduced himself and Sarah to the class, for some reason a scene from the 'Rocky and Bullwinkle Show' came to mind and I felt like I was in the presence of Boris Badenov and Natasha Fatale.

"Good morning class. My name is Lenny and this is Sarah. Welcome to the Horst Institute. You are here because your mothers could not teach you how to become hairdressers. This school isn't for everyone but it might be for you - We'll see," he stated, while looking directly at me.

I only met this guy five minutes ago and I already feel like I owe him an apology. I felt an instant case of introduction remorse was beginning to set in. Some things in life can be an inconvenient truth and I pray this isn't one of them.

"Sarah and I will be your instructors for the Alpha Phase of Basic here at the Institute. This is an eight week program that each student must complete satisfactorily before moving on to the next phase of training, which is Beta. The Alpha Phase will cover the basic fundamentals of hair design, cutting, perming, and color. We will begin this week discussing the sanitation and hygiene rules as they apply to protect the health of our students and the clients who are here for our services. We will also study the state laws and requirements that are regulated by the State Board of Cosmetology."

Lenny held court for the next two hours and didn't miss a beat, while Sarah was silent and studied the class. She was a pro and knew every class was different. She and Lenny had worked together before and they were excellent for teaching the introductory phase of Alpha at the Institute. Lenny may have been the mouthpiece during class but one look into Sarah's dark eyes and you could tell who the head honcho was.

Just before lunch our class got a surprise visit from 'Mr. Big' himself. Horst Rechelbacher dropped in to say hello and welcome us to the Institute along with his sidekick, Jose Ebér, who was hanging out for the day with Horst here in Minneapolis. I didn't have a clue who the hell Jose Ebér was and neither did anyone else in the class. If we did, the entire class would have lined up and asked for his autograph on our textbooks. Jose Ebér was a superstar in the beauty industry and a personal hairstylist for countless movie stars in Hollywood and around the world. He had a good gig going on and who knows, maybe he could luck out one day like Jon Peters and find himself directing and producing movies. He definitely had the style and personality for it.

Horst had already been a superstar in the beauty industry for many years. He was a local celebrity who was well known nationally and internationally as a gifted and talented artist and he had his sights set on some really big things now. He was quite the wordsmith when it came to promoting his Aveda product line and wellness concepts for the human race and the environment of our planet. He was like a New Age monk who had something that everybody wanted to be a part of. As far as he was concerned, Aveda was the way life should be lived and how the world should be run. Hell, he could have pissed in a pop bottle, called it holy water, and his devotees would have blessed themselves with it and believed it to be so.

Lenny finally checked out the wall clock and mumbled the words we were all waiting to hear. "Okay class, it's lunchtime. We'll meet back here in an hour. Hold on to your time cards. Sarah and I will sign them for you at the end of the day."

There were three things I needed right away, a bathroom, a

cigarette, and food. I was able to find all three at Jim's Café across the street. Some of us decided to sit together and do lunch while getting to know each other a little. It was the usual - who are you, what do you do and why are you here stuff. I ended up sharing a table with three cute ladies that were in my class. Lunch was also a good time to step out of my comfort zone and find out a little more about the people around me. We all had school in common and that meant we would be seeing each other nearly every day so establishing friendly relationships that I felt comfortable with was a smart thing to do.

For a straight guy like me, the thought of going to a beauty school could be a fun place to be but was not without it's problems. The first thing everybody thinks is that you are gay. It's the stereotype of a male hairdresser. I have all those TV shampoo commercials to thank for that!

That's just the way it is. As a male hairdresser, no matter where are, you can feel the curiosity of "Is he or isn't he?" It's the male counterpart of "Does she or doesn't she?", only the hairdresser knows for sure. Your only saving grace is to start mating with as many heifers on the farm as possible so the word gets out fast about what side of the fence you play on.

Lunch was over, another cigarette was done, and it was time to head back to school. As we made our way back to the classroom Sarah was watching us as we returned to our seats. She was quiet for the moment, as though she was clairvoyant and reading the thoughts of her student audience. I found myself wondering what was behind this veil of thought before us. She reminded me of a tarot card, the Queen of Swords. Her presence revealed the gift of a kind nature that was built on the knowledge of rougher times and the experience of some damn hard things. She knew how to express herself without letting you know what she was really thinking. She figured some of us had gotten to know each other a bit during lunch, and she was right. Sarah had her own way of getting to know people and she was so cool about it. Making other people feel important is an art and an attitude, which she enjoyed. I believe it was a daily practice that she would continue to cultivate for the rest of her life. With a smile as deep as the color of her eyes, Sarah asked "Let me guess - lunch at Jim's, right?"

Most of us gave her the nod.

"I eat there a lot. The food's good and I enjoy the company of the students around me."

I had the feeling that something was coming and we were being set up and didn't know it.

"One of the things I enjoy after a good lunch is how I'm ready to start the day again. A hot meal, a cup of coffee and a cigarette has a way of putting things back into perspective for me."

After hearing this, now I knew why I always wanted a cigarette after sex. Wow! What insight this woman has. From what I had experienced at lunch today she was right on. Sarah understood the power of style and hers radiated from the depth of her soul. She never needed a trendy addition to freshen up. Her classic repertoire was in good taste and always enough.

"We have a class of twenty here and that's about the average. What I like about a class this size is that it gives Lenny and myself more time to work with each student individually. We get to know you better and this helps us to address the needs of the class as a whole. I would like to ask each student to stand up, introduce yourself and share with the class why you are here. I will begin by calling out your student ID number. When your number is called please stand."

I can tell you that I was nervous as hell about standing up and introducing myself before my number was called. Shit! What was I gonna say? I needed a good lie fast. It sure as hell wasn't going to be the truth of being a screw up and just getting out of a Rehab Center in Baltimore.

Sarah began calling out numbers and the names stood up with the faces telling their stories.

This class was a mixed bag with a wide spectrum of individuals who were now here as students. I wasn't surprised that I saw no Doctors, Lawyers or Indian Chiefs. We did have our share of those born with a silver spoon up their ass but they were young and their days of being spoon fed were not over yet. Sarah was able to read between the lines of each story and so was I. Some of the students were here due to the response of being damaged and broken in some way. Many in this room were the survivors of the things life had asked of them and not what they had wished for from life. Like myself, after a lot of therapy and rehab, this place was a redemption and a second chance. A new start with a clean slate after surviving a bad scene and a new tomorrow which had already begun this morning in a new place that offered support, guidance, promise and hope in an atmosphere of reasonable compassion.

Sarah called number 129. Standing up and being real didn't seem like a hard thing to do now and I felt like I was sharing about myself, which for some reason seemed different than exposing myself. I learned a long time ago not to put a whole lot of energy in trying to fit in. I always ended up standing out in some way. It's just who I am, so why not embrace it instead of worry about it? Sooner or later the truth would come out that I wasn't very much of a conformist. It was time to let my wit and gift of gab lead the way.

"My name is Joe and my nickname is Dustin. I got that because a lot of people I knew said I reminded of them of Dustin Hoffman." The class laughed out loud and some of them remarked that I did. "Like you, I'm here because our mothers could not teach us how to become hairdressers. I've always liked the idea of working with hair and I was told by many people in this field that the Horst Institute was the best school in the country for becoming a hairdresser, so I guess I can say I'm here prospecting for the club."

I was the last number up and that made it easier for me. Why? Because I realized that as a class we had so much in common. I felt a connection of being with people who had experienced life in so many ways other than those who grew up as trust fund babies who were still sucking on the tit of a privileged lifestyle, and so did Sarah. She ended the class by signing our time cards and letting us know to meet here in the same room at 7:45 am tomorrow.

My first day here at school was over and in the bank. With some notes and a few reading assignments, I was on my way home. Like any other class, we mixed and mingled together. When the day was over I remembered the things I said and heard that made me want to cringe. I didn't dwell on the imperfections of it - no big deal, besides that's what makes us humans so charming.

The walk back through Dinkytown to the Frat Shack was just as cold as it had been this morning but in my head I knew I was going home with something besides cold ears and a notebook. I knew that twice a day I was going to and from the places I was supposed to be and I was happy with that. I felt lucky. When I first came here I had no idea how much I was going to change and how much things were going to matter in my life again someday. I felt like I was exploring a different culture, though not the ways of those from another country. This was the culture of health, balance and happiness. Some people never find the places and the times they wished for and dreamed of, but I had. It was real and it felt amazing!

Were you robbing the cradle?

No, I wouldn't say that,

it was more like I had succumbed

to the needs of the elderly.

Chapter 9: Hairballs

We have a saying here in this country that if you're poor and needy this is one of the best places in the world to find yourself down and out.

So I guess it stands to reason, if you're a poor student attending an expensive school, having a close friend like Randy would mean a lot. Living in a Jewish Frat Shack might just be the best situation one could hope for and this was the place I was in. There was a Mezuzah on the left side of the door frame at the entrance of the house. For the people who lived here it was a constant reminder of God's presence and good deeds. This was always reflected in the way I was treated and respected as a fellow student in the house. I've been very lucky since I have been here. I'm doing well in a great school and I've made a few friends along the way. Those two things alone were reason enough for me to feel really good about coming here to Minneapolis. With some damn rough times far behind me now, I had come to believe this symbol of God's compassion to be true. Hell, I was even kissing it with my own two fingers while going in and out the door.

Here in the States the color of money is green. As far as the hair care product industry was concerned, Aveda had become the new green giant. You can bet your sweet ass that Horst Rechelbacher was singing "Ho, Ho, Ho" all the way to the bank. The Horst Institute was the number one school in the country for training in the field of cosmetology and, perhaps, it was the number one school in the world as well. Contrary to popular belief, beauty school was no easy walk in the park, certainly not here. Life at the Institute was a forty hour a week job. This didn't count the additional hours for homework and related school projects.

Randy had cut me a sweet deal on the rent in return for the cleaning services I performed here at the house, which left little or no time at all for moonlighting at a second job. My lean times were the direct result of the Veterans Administration's failure to send a school check to the bank because of some incompetent, bureaucratic idiot who had misplaced my paperwork. This, in turn, created a six week delay for me getting paid. As students at a university or a private school, like the one I'm attending, we all share the same kind of stakes. When it comes to lost checks or delayed funds for school we can end up with a boot in the ass as we are shown to the door. This could be the life or death of a future career and nobody's numb to life and death. I felt like a sitting duck whose ass was shit out of luck and enduring a very piss poor state of affairs. I was so angry at the government that I just couldn't wait to see some dead presidents buried deep down in my wallet next to my ass.

Everybody enjoys a good time, especially when we've got life by the balls and everything is rolling our way, but right now I felt like life was busting mine. My best days were usually spent doing whatever I wanted to do. This seems impossible now as I look around and see all the things I should be doing. I wish I could give myself permission to ignore the 'shoulds' in favor of spending some quality time with my heathen ways for a much needed break.

At the Institute, titles meant little to me unless it was a name tag on a lapel that read 'Instructor'. For the most part, they were very dedicated and worthy of respect and admiration. I've seen them stay after school for hours just to help a student gain clarity and mastery with a challenging task or project. The pursuit of excellence was the mission statement for instructors and students alike here at the Horst Institute.

No place is perfect and there were a couple of wild cards here who challenged my ability, at times, to keep my cool. I felt they used their office and position as a power trip over some of the students just to satisfy their own egos. Pam and Lenny were two such parasites that rode on the backs of others they felt were below receiving their good graces. Where I came from this was known as jawboning and it was everything I could do to hold back my tongue during some stressful situations with these two. Even a small run in with any authority figure here could leave you soul searching to seek life elsewhere. Sometimes no matter how hard I would try to be nice, my eyes would still go snaky at anyone who pissed me off, but as long as I kept my mouth shut and my thoughts to myself there was never a problem.

My issues with Pam and Lenny should not have been such a big deal because I've seen this show before and I knew how this rerun was going to end. The skin on my ass was thick and in no way was I going to sweat the small stuff, like wannabe bullies pushing wolf tickets. Hell was nothing new for me. I had been there many times and as far as I was concerned it was nothing more than a place to reevaluate the situation and move on.

Randy, the house manager and now a good friend, said "Don't worry about the rent. We'll settle up when you get paid". I was cutting Randy's hair once a week at ten dollars a clip just to keep myself in cigarettes and coffee. It was his way of helping me out. Randy always made it a point to show off my handiwork and it wasn't long before I was cutting all the heads in the house. Besides the benefit of having lunch money, this was another way of getting to know the guys in the house. Soon I was being invited to hang out with the boys in the house at such places as the Peanut Bar around the Ragstock area of Dinkytown and the more expensive hot spots over on the East Bank.

My world had made another turn, and things were working out well. I was fine with everything just the way it was. But Randy was a man of vision and when it came to money he could see the future faster than a gypsy. In the basement of the Frat Shack there was an old laundry room that was no longer in use. That was until now.

It was the perfect place for a shop - a hair shop that is. It had an old utility sink and florescent lighting. We found an old barber chair for free, just for hauling it away from an abandoned house in north Minneapolis. We took out the utility sink and replaced it with a used shampoo bowl and with a fresh paint job, the place was coming together.

Randy advanced me a few hundred dollars to purchase the stuff I needed to get the shop up and running. We named it 'The Bootleg Salon'. It was illegal , it was underground, and it was a hit. The success formula is the same today as it was yesterday. Imagination plus work, equaled freedom and a cool change. The difference is I was getting better at both things in a positive and specific way. The heads that were wearing my cuts starting catching eyes and began dropping dimes about The Bootleg Salon in the basement at the bottom of the Frat Shack. The beauty of The Bootleg Salon was that it presented a situation with no rules. This was a perfect chance for me to establish my own standards of what worked for me and the hell with what didn't. What else could be better than that? My business card simply read "Hair Done Neat and Cheap".

The Bootleg was doing so well I had to bring in another student stylist from the Institute just to keep up with the work. His name was Arthur and we were classmates at the Institute and I knew that we could work together comfortably. Arthur was better with the chemical services and I was a bit sharper with the cuts. So Arthur did all the perms, colors, and foils while I performed all cuts, styling and design consultations. We were a good team and it was fun.

We were getting work, paid and laid! Whoever said "Never get your meat and bread from the same store" was full of shit. We were booked on Sundays and Mondays, ten hours a day easy, and during the late evening hours of the school week sometimes we finished up as late as 1:00 a.m. After paying Arthur a 50% commission for the services performed on his clients 'tax free' and the cost of supplies,

Randy and I did a 70/30 percent split and he was satisfied with the smaller amount. It was all cash, tax free, drug free and with no ATF concerns.

Some of the students from the U of M were sorority sisters who knew about The Bootleg Salon at the Frat Shack and were hip to the idea of the work being done cheap and done neat by two guys in a house on Frat Row. Soon The Bootleg Salon had more sorority sisters getting haircuts than the fraternities had getting laid. I was making more money right here where I lived than I'd ever made in my life. Arthur and I were literally up to our necks in hair and ass.

By this time my checks from the Veterans Administration were coming in on a monthly basis while I was attending the Institute on my GI Bill. My first check was huge and it included four months of back pay. Wow! That just might be enough for a down payment to get my ass in a new car. I was making some good cash with The Bootleg Salon, so why not? I went downtown and checked out an uptown car, a black Formula Firebird that was loaded. That ride was sitting on the showroom floor looking like a high class hooker that was ready to show me a good time. It didn't take long for a salesman to see that it was love at first sight with this car and I, so he approached me like a smooth pimp decked out in a $200 suit and put out his pitch. "I think you and this car were made for each other. You both have a style that stands out. So, what do you think? Let's run the numbers and see if we can get you hooked up. My name is Ed. Let's take a walk to my desk and see if we have a match, or perhaps you might be interested in one of our other models."

Ed and I sat down together and it was time for me to put on one of my best shows. The only thing standing between me and the car of my dreams was the paperwork - a credit application. Ed and I filled out that app together using my best bullshit, staying as close to the truth as possible. A $2500 down payment was chump change to me now but without a credit approval from a bank my chances of getting that car were zilch. We completed the paperwork and I cut him a check. Because today was Saturday, it would be Tuesday or Wednesday before we heard back from the bank. That was fine with me because it was going to take a few days for me to come up with some real unheard of shit that would cover my ass. That car was curbside cool and if I was going to get it, I had some homework to do before Ed phoned me with the lowdown from the bank.

To start with, I got a letter from my bank stating that I was receiving electronic deposits from the Department of Defense. It was addressed "To Whom It May Concern" at the dealership. I asked my bank not to disclose the amount of money I was receiving because I felt it was personal. Because my request made sense it wasn't a problem. As far as the dealership was concerned, I was receiving monthly deposits as a retiree of the DOD and not that of a student who was attending a beauty school.

It was Wednesday and still no word from the dealership so I just figured the bank said "No fucking way" and I would get a denial letter in the mail. Then the phone rang. It was Ed on the line. "Joe, we got it done but the bank is a little on the fence about it so if you can come in tonight I need you to bring in everything you can to verify the information we submitted on your credit application."

"No problem, Ed. Will six p.m. work?"

"Yeah Joe, we're open until ten tonight. If everything is good we'll have you in your new wheels before then."

Along with the letter from my bank showing the monthly deposits from the DOD, I gathered up a few months of bank statements showing deposits of cash and checks from The Bootleg Salon, of which I stated that I owned. I didn't feel the need to explain that it was in the basement of a Frat House. I gave them a business card with an address that matched my drivers license and bank statement along with a valid phone number and things were cool.

As luck would have it, Ed was just as manipulative and cunning as I was. He wanted to do the deal as much as I did so with some of his underhanded cleverness we came together on the terms and made it happen. He made a sale with a good commission and I held the keys to my first brand new car. He wanted to give me the low down on the car and all it's features, but I didn't have time for that bullshit.

Believe me, when I sat in that car and turned it on, it was built to return the favor. The instruments and controls lit up a deep red against the black face panels. The stereo came to life with a hit song from Prince and the purr of that engine was throaty and deep. The thrill I felt driving off, surrounded by the scent of new car leather, was beyond words. This car was mine and so were the payments of $285 a month for the next sixty months. So what? I had forty five days and plenty of heads to cut before the first payment was due, and right now I felt like I was living out loud.

On the way back to the house I stopped at a bar for a drink and a cigarette. I ordered a scotch and soda with a lemon twist, fired up a Marlboro Red and just relaxed happily while reflecting on how much had changed in such a short time. Things were good at school, at home, and with me. I lived in a house with students, who had become good friends, and Randy, who felt like a brother.

A waitress came up to the bar and asked "Can I help you with something else?"

I just said "No thank you sweetheart, I'm good." I smiled because these words had a real meaning for me now.

Randy and I were now sharing the largest apartment in the Frat Shack, which we called 'The Penthouse'. It had three rooms and a real fireplace and across the hall was The Bootleg Salon. It was Saturday and that meant another kegger was happening at the house tonight. I took the liberty of inviting a few friends from the Institute to come over and hang out. This was a good scene and I wanted to share it with some of my friends from school. Johnson was working the turntable like a pro while Randy was working the door checking fake ID cards and charging five bucks a head to get in. Tommy was tapping the beer kegs and any ass he could get his rat claws on at the same time, and if that didn't work out he could always call up his old lady at the end of the night.

Tommy was a dental student at the U of M and was living a double life. One during the week as a student while staying at the Frat Shack and the other on weekends with his wife and kid at home. He came across as a very devoted family man at home. That was smart on his part considering that his wife's parents were footing the bill for his education. When it came to women, Tommy had talent despite the fact that he wasn't charming, funny or tall. He did have charisma and that was enough for him to marry into money. In Tommy's head, the end justified the means. After graduation and a divorce, child support was still cheaper to fork over than the payments of some costly school loans, and besides it was tax deductible and interest free. What can I say? He was a dental student and he was always looking for a cavity someplace to drill and fill.

It was the weekend - a time to let go and hang out. As the night wore on the party became one big scavenger hunt for booty. Everybody was doing their own thing and that included eating, drinking, dancing, screwing, and sleeping if everything worked out according to plan.

A few friends of mine from the Institute showed up and I was happy to see them. Sandy, who was in my class at school, brought a friend by the name of Sharon. She was a student who was set to graduate next month. She was twenty three with red hair, green eyes, and the look of being born of good stock. We had seen each other at school on a few occasions but this was the first time we had talked and we were getting to know each other. After spending some time with her, I could tell I didn't need to make a decision between personality and character over position and pedigree. By most standards I was considered an old guy for attending a beauty school and living in a Frat House. This may have been the truth but that didn't mean I couldn't act on a hot hunch when I felt one. There was chemistry and a bio match here, and she was a total package.

Tommy managed to hook up with Sandy that night and Randy was doing a sleep over with Kate, as usual. For me, after a slow dance with Sharon, she leaned over and whispered in my ear "Would I mind sleeping in tomorrow?" I was thirty eight years old and at a time like this, I considered myself to be some low hanging fruit that was ripe and ready. Hell, nobody was going to need a ladder to reach for me. Sharon was wild in a classy way and a sweetheart all wrapped up in one. She had the charm of a mature woman with the look of innocence in her eyes and on her face. When the party ended, she slept over and I woke up around 4:30 in the morning with a curvy redhead next to me. She kissed me softly and closed her eyes and I just stared at her for a few moments while thinking how good it felt to be here. I had a beautiful gal next to me and a house full of friends. It doesn't get any better than this!

Sometimes I've wondered

why some people just never seem to get it,

until I finally figured it out!

It was because they never knew

what they really wanted,

and were too focused on the things

they never had,

while staying on a path

that never changed.

Chapter 10: Riff Raff's Revenge

The kegger over the weekend was one hell of a good time and definitely one that would go down in the record book as a keeper. It's 5:30 a.m. again, a quiet and comfortable time now for a cigarette and the aroma therapy of a fresh cup of coffee before making my way to the shower. Like most mornings, I'm slowly doing one thing at a time until I walk out the door and then it's ... BAM ... People Shock ... Buses ... Car Horns ... Bicycles ... Coffee Lines ... Lights ... Action ... Voices ... Me...

It took a while but I developed the ability to reach a balance during these turbulent times. Most people concentrate far too much on life and there's no need to. Even after all these years there's so much that I don't have covered in my own life and it's hard to understand the whole thing and what it means. All we really need to do is just live it as simply and as effortlessly as possible. I made peace with it by meditating on the thought that these were simply the sounds of life saying "Good morning, Joe!"

Getting up early has become easier than it was when I first came here from Baltimore. Thank goodness most of the cold weather and snow have finally passed. The blue skies and warm, sunny days were much more of what I was accustomed to. So much has changed in just three short months and the meaning of my life is something I have come to know a lot better. My sense of timing was slightly ahead of most people. My time management skills had been honed over the many years I spent in Rehab Centers and I tend to get more accomplished than others, especially when I'm in a pinch. The downside of this is that I'm prone to frustration due to the excruciatingly slow pace of others that sometimes gets in the way of my best efforts.

I still have my bells from hell, jackhammer alarm clock. I keep it around as a prank to use when someone is sleeping over. It rattled Sharon's ass so bad one morning that she jumped like hell out of bed thinking it was a fire alarm. Sometimes I think it's funny because it does have a fast way of getting a sleepover's ass up and out the door. After all, I've got my own schedule to deal with and time management rules when you are a student at the Institute. The Alpha Phase of training at the Institute is ending this week. It's a very important time for us students and it is also known as "Hell Week", full of practical finals and various multiple choice tests. For students this week at the Institute, there's no time for beers and cheers or ass on the grass in the valley of the dolls. We needed every hour to prepare ourselves for the challenges which will be presented to us as a class by the instructors of the Institute.

There are times at the Institute when all the rules and social dynamics can become exhausting. There are a lot of easygoing people here, and some who are likely to assess the correctness of your every move. I could tell that a few of the instructors here needed to get a life, besides their job. Some of them could be so anal and dogmatic at times, it could drive a student up a wall. I just wanted to keep on creating whatever felt good to me without anyone's input as to how I should or shouldn't be doing it.

Arthur and I have decided to close The Bootleg Salon for a week. We felt we needed the time to concentrate solely on the task of doing well on our exams and completing the Alpha Phase of training. We spent most of the week at the Frat Shack preparing ourselves for the various multiple choice tests of our finals. We were reading over and over, again and again, the rules of sanitation and hygiene with the laws and regulations of the State Board of Cosmetology. It was a lot of boring, bureaucratic small print stuff to remember with numbers and symbols that neither one of us had ever seen before, but we had better know it on examination day and that was tomorrow.

The night passed fast, the morning was here and we were in class listening to the final instructions that were given before testing by Sarah and Lenny. I knew Arthur and myself would do well with the practical applications of various permanent wave wraps, color, cutting, and multiple setting and comb out styling procedures. Everything we learned at the Institute was practiced by us at The Bootleg Salon in the Frat Shack. It was like getting paid cash for doing our homework and we were, BIG TIME.

Before Sarah became the School Manager of the Institute she had spent a great deal of time working with the fashion design industry. She may have stood on the sidelines but she knew how to talk and walk red carpet style with the best of them. With her notebook, pen and camera in hand she was a well known face in the crowd. Hair always follows fashion and that always explained her presence next to the runways of the New York and Paris design shows. She had seen a lot of the world and I think she was always ready for a pleasant surprise, especially from a creative student here at the Institute.

Lenny's claim to fame, as an instructor, was his outstanding talent for up do's and creative comb outs. He was an excellent speaker as well. As a roller set and comb out artist, he had found his niche and was one of the best in the state. If someone, or something, was going to hold on to his attention it was going to require a little something extra. Perhaps a bit of eccentricity, passion, or even a good novelty would do.

A finger wave with skip curls, or reverse waves done well with a curling iron, was an eye catching piece of art work for any instructor at the Institute. Sarah and Lenny had a classical background and an appreciation for these 1940's classic styles. These styles were often referred to as the jaguars of classic hair design. They were always fashionable and in good taste, and I knew it. Another thing I had in my corner was that Sarah and Lenny were also the acting examiners during the testing for the State Board of Cosmetology.

It can take a lot of balls to let one's creativity take off like this, but sometimes we just have to risk failure by leaving all the expected and normal limits behind. The cards I was holding now looked pretty good so why not take the gamble and besides, I was betting on myself to win. Playing it safe meant there was no place for a miracle to occur if I needed one. So I decided to take a long-shot with something I hoped they would like. I presented my hair design model wearing a classic reverse wave style with the outer perimeter flowing in skip curls. I also added a side parting, which began at the vertex of her head and angled just over the middle of the left eye. I knew that a strong beginning with an excellent finish could grant a student forgiveness for the sins of screwing something up in the middle of the stretch. The day before our showing I asked my model to arch her eyebrows, very close, and to pencil them thin, but dark before our presentation. She wore a vibrant red lipstick with no liner, which presented more of an era statement. I knew my work was good and worthy of standing on its own because I loved what I was doing and I knew that I looked good while I was doing it.

I had been taught a few lessons while being a guest at a Rehab Center in Baltimore which served me well as a student here in Minneapolis at the Institute. Dr. Hanson always reminded me that we are not the things we say, we are the things we do, and I found those words to be so true today.

Every private school has a number of students born with a silver spoon up their ass while sucking on the tit of entitlement and thinking it's something to die for. It is said that bad things often come in threes. It's true and they were all in my class. They were Lenny's groupies who became his class pets and I found them irritating as hell. I often referred to them as being the class spoons that Lenny would pull out of his ass from time to time as visual examples of professionalism and the ideal student image of the Institute. These gents were the walking, talking poster children of gay pride for the gay contingent here at school. They were polished, poised and well spoken, but their time had come today to show if they could truly shine. It was all show and no go. These trust fund babies had no idea of cutting hair like a scissor star but they definitely had the cool looking part of it down. This trio had even developed the pitch of a twenty four carat accent. Learning was the result of reinforced practice but that didn't mean standing in front of a mirror reciting "Mirror, mirror on the wall, who's the fairest of them all?" Any heads of hair that were sailing under these shears were definitely going to be scuttled today. There are a lot of pranksters in the beauty business and I believe it is the beauty schools that tend to breed them.

Hell week was over, testing was done and Alpha Phase had been completed. All the hard work paid off for Arthur and I. Now it was time to kick back and chill with a few high fives and a couple of beers. The past, present and future, known as the fates of life, were happy and so were we with our much earned success. All that was left was a final interview and evaluation by an instructor before moving on to the next phase at the Institute.

The Horst Institute was the number one school in the country as an educational center for the field of Cosmetology. Like any private school, it was very expensive to attend and the price of this privilege was reflected in your checkbook and felt on your social calendar. From the start of week one, the next fifty two Saturdays were no longer your own. Just like your school grant was the property of the Institute, the participation and presence of your ass was a school requirement. Saturday's hangovers, for most of us, were the sins of Friday's parties and sleepovers without much sleep. If you could tough it out until lunch time at Jim's Café, you could slide and survive through the rest of the day.

Liberty passes on Saturdays were few and far between at the Institute and short of another "My grandmother just died" story or a very special act of God, you were shit out of luck. I never missed a Saturday, no matter what. It was one thing to show up with a clinic slip and a fake STD bullshit story for the short office visit at school, because it was such a personal matter that no one would question it. It was another thing explaining that to the Veterans Administration, who was footing my tuition for school. I didn't want or need that kind of heat coming down on me.

Today was Saturday and it was the one that we as a class had been waiting for. Somehow even our trust fund, whirling dervish gents had completed Alpha and passed with the rest of our class. For some it was a reward of their hard work and efforts, and for others just the dumb luck of divine intervention helping those who couldn't help themselves.

Our class had only one thing on the schedule today and that was a brief evaluation interview with Lenny. His stamp of approval was an essential necessity - without it could mean repeating the Alpha Phase all over again. Then the rest of the day was ours. After waiting a while it was finally my turn to sit and have a chat with Lenny. I always thought of Lenny as being a very passive aggressive instructor whenever he was working with me. He had a way of letting you know that you were still a piece of work and by no means a work of art yet.

He was one of those people who knew how to ask good questions, but really sucked at listening, especially if the response wasn't the one he wanted to hear. At times, his sharp tongue was enough to send a student to the school office to file a complaint. His approach to teaching was the exact opposite of Sarah's. Her attraction secrets were simple. She always knew how to inspire people to feel good about themselves whenever she was around them. Her intensity was always set on high but she was never overbearing. Sarah's energy was pleasantly effective and her attributes as a teacher touched many of the students here at the Institute in a positive manner.

"Mr. Ross, please come in and sit down."

I could already tell from the tone of his voice that this interview was in no way going to end as a prize winning review for work well done. "Mr. Ross, you have a creative rawness within your talent as a stylist that will serve you well once it has become aged with grace, experience, guidance, and confidence instead of beginners dumb luck and your street smart ways. At times I have found your rude manner and impoliteness to be despicable and inconsiderate of me in the presence of my class but your hard work and strategic, manipulative ways have won the day for you and I suspect you will do well."

I was beginning to feel like the "you've got to be kidding me" winds were blowing my way. Unlike the hair that had stopped growing on his head, the irritation I felt for this instructor was still growing in mine, and he was quickly becoming what felt like a thorn in my ass. Some people make a hell of a lot out of a hell of a little and this was one of those times. Lenny's problem wasn't about my need for going to the bathroom. I was never gone more than three minutes and I was always polite by quietly leaving the room and returning. Lenny's bitch was that I never raised my hand and asked permission to leave the room. It was because of this that he felt I was impolite, ill-mannered and rude. He had held on to this stupid shit for three months until it had now become a poker chip that he was going to cash in today to bite my ass with at this moment. If this drama queen had a problem with me for not raising my hand when I needed to take a piss, he should have said something from day one. I had always respected his authority as our instructor, but liberty is a soul's right to breathe and in some situations that just might include an unauthorized piss break. The smart thing to do with this guy was to stay on sacred ground and that place was never crossing the line of his authority. The wrong words from a student's pie hole could result in a pen whipping faster than a New York minute.

I was always mindful of the content of my communications to, or about, any of the instructors here at the Institute, especially with this one at the moment because he had not yet signed off on my evaluation. This may have been a time to kiss ass and fast, but I preferred thinking of it as success disguised as a sacrifice. So I thanked him for his insight and guidance while reminding him that I was still a worthy piece of work in progress. Thank God, these must have been the words he was waiting to hear. Finally, my time sitting on the pot with Lenny, holding my review work like shit papers, ended after an hour of what should have been a 10-minute sign and go in peace interview.

In the end we both got what we wanted. My review was signed favorably and red penned by Lenny that he suspected I would do well in the future. Of course, this only occurred after I had given him an extorted apology for my perceived rudeness during his class for failing to raise my hand and ask permission when I needed to take a bathroom break. He was sneaky, geeky, and creepy. When I left his office I felt like I had removed myself from the hole of a serpent.

Academically speaking, the morning had been somewhat of a chilly start but my social life was about to warm up real soon. I had met a new face in the crowd at school named Kara. We would shoot the shit from time to time over a cup of coffee and one day I thought "Why not ask her out?" Everything is hit or miss and maybe this would turn out be one of those God things. It was a short day for both of us at school so we decided to have lunch and check out the night life at the bars in Dinkytown later that evening. Kara was easy on the eyes and just as smooth to get along with. She had the look and softness of a pink satin pillow that was evenly matched with a sensitive courage and together came across as a whole helluva lot of hot. Sometimes just drinking coffee with her I had felt the blush of lust on my school boy face, hoping my smile was hiding some of my shyness. It embarrassed me a little, but she thought it was hilarious.

There was good chemistry between the two of us with every hour that passed. It was a fun date and not once did I find myself asking where the excitement was because it was with us in everything we did. The night ended with a few beers at the Peanut Bar, a walk home and a goodnight kiss. This had been a cool day in my life when everything I wanted to happen did. It had been a whole day, like the wholeness of life, starting in drama and ending with the beginning of a newly found love story.

As I walked home to the Frat Shack, I passed through Dinkytown once more and looked across the street at the Peanut Bar. It had been a fun place full of cigarette smoke, loud music and cold beer while Kara and I sat facing each other on bar stools blowing smoke rings in the air with our cigarettes. We were talking good shit about the things we liked and like most people, we were talking bullshit about the things that we didn't.

Somewhere there's a someone for everyone but for the short term the no ties, low maintenance, of a real nobody was better to make do with than the high profile of commitment required to maintain the needs of a real somebody. Why put ourselves out? We were students having a good time instead of being on a scavenger hunt for a trophy mate. That happy shit was for the Frats and Sororities at the U of M. Life here at the Institute was more avant garde and we were a bit more spontaneous, creating whatever we felt inspired by at the moment.

Kara and I began hanging out a lot together and it made attending the Institute more pleasurable than it had been in the past. When two people can share the same cigarette it was just another way of swapping spit but on a higher level it was a token of trust and an act of closeness, especially when seen in the presence of others.

Sometimes the "me and my stories" of people can screw up the potential of a good relationship ASAP, but this was never a problem with us. Why? Because we were smart enough not to go there.

Bringing up bad scenes from the past were a downer. It was like calling back the dead and pretending they were no longer zombies. We had each other now and that was enough redemption for us.

Screwed up haircuts were one thing, but screwed up heads from the matters of the heart were another. The drama of beauty school romance and puppy love gone bad was a real tear jerking scene. There were always some broken hearts around here and I saw this as a business opportunity. I had been reading tarot cards for a few years. It was something I enjoyed doing and I was good at it. The word got around fast at school that I was hip with the cards and the lip service was paying me fifteen dollars a reading for students and twenty for instructors.

People go to therapists and card readers for the same reasons and a big one is because they can't deal well with conflict and uncertainty. The situations people usually desire more clarity with are about relationships, health, money, and legal problems.

One time I did a reading for an instructor concerning the theft of a large amount of money at the Institute. Most of the cards were laying out reversed and no matter what spread I used, the Seven of Swords always had a way of showing up. This indicated a lot of lies or a lot of secrets and the fear of imprisonment or addiction along with a hefty dose of confusion about the situation. I wasn't sure what to make of this reading because it wasn't a fit for the person I thought I knew. They weren't giving me the real story. They were saying one thing but the cards were saying another. Sooner or later the truth comes out in the wash.

For reasons unknown at the time, they were soon released from the Institute without any advance notice. It was like one day they were here and the next, like a fart in the wind... gone. I found out later this instructor was a coke addict and had fabricated the theft in hopes of scoring some pity money from the Institute, or possibly a fraudulent insurance claim.

In truth the instructor was a sweetheart of a person who got caught up in some bad shit and I hoped down the road things had worked out, and they did. A while later I was checking out the news on the TV and there they were as a reporter and news anchor. I thought "Good for you. Everybody deserves a second chance. No one's future should be condemned because of the sins of their past."

Sometimes the card readings cut into my time with Kara but she didn't mind because we usually did something after school anyway. Kara asked me a few times to read her cards but I declined because I preferred not knowing anything about her that she would not have told me herself. Sometimes falling in love with the right person can help show who you are without a card telling you so. There are some people that we experience as gifts in our lives and the feelings of those moments are far beyond what words could ever describe.

At school I had been flipping a lot of cards on the love lives of others so I decided to flip one on my own. Up came the card of the Tower, Number 16, and it's message was to expect the unexpected. There was no way to read this card because there is no way to prepare for the possible situation one might encounter as a lesson in life. It was one of those "wait and see" things and there is nothing you can do but wait for it.

Kara and I were sitting together one morning during a lecture at the Institute from a guest speaker of a very successful salon here in Minneapolis. He began his lecture with the mission statement of his salon. "We do not hire hairdressers at our salon. We hire personalties who are committed to becoming successful craftsmen for an industry that is hungry for talented artists. We demand and expect nothing less than the pursuit of excellence from all of our staff, for all of our clients, all of the time."

After hearing this lecture from a guy who looked like Sebastian Cabot, I whispered to Kara that I might want to make some changes to my business cards regarding The Bootleg Salon from "hair done neat and cheap" to "pay like hell for hair done well". She just chuckled and whispered "I need to talk with you today at lunchtime."

I could tell by the look on her face that something was up and it was important to her.

After the lecture she gave me a fast peck on the cheek and said "We'll talk about it later." I felt like some weird shit was about to come down on me.

I met Kara at Jim's Café and we sat at our usual table. Kara was about to reveal a sensitive and sticky situation regarding our relationship. After a silent moment, she said "Joseph, I care about you and I know our relationship is going someplace but there is something I have to share with you. I have been wanting to tell you this for a long time now but I was afraid of hurting your feelings. There is something I have been keeping from you and that you have to know about me."

Here comes the bomb and just before it blew, I prepared myself with a thought that she was either pregnant or married. I wasn't even close and there was some real undercover shit coming my way. "OK Kara, let's have it. What's up?"

"Joseph, I'm bisexual."

I knew she wasn't joking but I had to ask her anyway. "Kara, is this some kind of a joke?"

"No it isn't. I'm sorry I want to work this out between us some way and continue our relationship because I care about you."

I just sat there and didn't know how to respond with any words I felt I could say. I felt the double take of a bewildered expression hit my face. I wasn't crushed and I wasn't lost, but I was stunned and in an emotional stupor. If there was ever a time to assess our relationship from a different angle it was now. There was nothing I could do. I left Kara sitting there alone even though I knew she was hurting, too, but there wasn't anything I could give to her or myself, except for my absence from what had now become a very uncomfortable scene.

The Frat Shack was full of friends, including my best one, Randy, but all I wanted to do was just to be alone. If you can't make yourself available for others then why the hell start up in the first place? Nothing hurts more than the pain of an emotional bitch slap to the heart.

Kara and I were supposed to be doing a movie tonight but I wasn't in the mood to be sharing popcorn with anyone, especially now. My head was still in the clouds over Kara's coming out surprise for me today. My thoughts regarding it were like a hung jury that was still in a closed session and a verdict had not yet been reached. There must be a way to coexist and interact with this situation that's fair, but what?

Kara was just being Kara and that meant just being honest and direct with me. In her mind she thought it was the only fair thing to do when you're a bisexual lady and dating a guy. She had taken a risk and now the ball was in my court. I was thinking one thing and feeling another, so what? This was nothing new. It was the way men had always responded to women since the beginning of time. A lesson from therapy was to go with my gut in a situation like this and my gut was telling me that I loved Kara. The sea of love had become a little wavy to say the least, but it was in no way a threat to my emotional survival and no reason to jump ship yet.

Situations like this have a way of working themselves out sooner or later. All of a sudden it was Bang, Bang, Bang on my door at the Frat Shack. It sounded like the cops and when I answered the door it was Kara. I was happy to see her and in no way did I want her out of my life. But why was she here at my door?

"Joe, can I come in and speak with you because I wasn't trying to push you away today."

I gave her a tight hug and a long kiss and said "Let's sit down and talk for awhile. The café may not have been the best place for this today."

It wasn't like I had to cannibalize who I was and become a wax figure of some kind that would allow me to be less self conscious of myself for dating a two sided lady like Kara. I needed to live and let live instead of sweating the small stuff. I made us some coffee and we smoked a few butts. We decided to work this issue out some way because Kara and I wanted to give this thing a chance.

For a good while Kara and I were running damn smooth together as a couple, with the least amount of problems most of the time. Even with some of the two sided stuff we had to deal with, what the hell? We were still looking cool together.

Just like people, love can come and go, live and die. Kara and I were like the toys that life had chosen to play with for awhile. It was fun and one of the best times of my school days at the Institute. Kara and I were like the wild flowers over a landscape that every so often occurs between two people from two very different places in life and in love. Dating someone who isn't right for you in the long run is just as stupid as sleeping with someone you feel the ultimate discomfort with. Unconditional love for one another does not mean short changing the standards you have set for yourself. Kara and I knew in our hearts this beautiful and rare tie we shared together was for the here and now, and not for the place we called the later and then. When the tea leaves finally settled for her and I, the message was very clear. We can't always finish the things that we helped to start. Some things are meant to be abandoned mid way. We both learned about who we were and what we were not from our experience together, and maybe that was the whole point to begin with. At the end of the day, we chose to accept the things we could live with in our lives and we were both smart enough to let go and walk away from the things that we couldn't.

The tarot card of the Tower was correct in its message to expect the unexpected. I was the reader and the messenger of the prophesy that was here now and fulfilled. When it comes to the needs of the heart, we all want an angle to play. Looking back now, I see that it was the old dream of a love affair which had become the good dream of a romance that just didn't work out.

THE PEACE AND LOVE VIBES

OF

TRUTH AND SOUL INCORPORATED

Chapter 11: Scoundrels, Trophy Wives, and Creepy Cheats

B ecause of my age and life experience, sometimes I felt like a role model of some kind in the eyes of others whether I wanted to be or not. But that's okay, I didn't mind being observed. As far as I was concerned it helped me to step up my game. A lot of times those with less experience were watching senior students, like myself, to pick up on some cues for how they should behave and perform on the cutting floor here at the Institute. It's a good thing to take pride in your work, especially when it has been done with grace and skill. The skill part of this true story might be a bit of a stretch but it did happen and I'm gonna own up to it. There was a day when my head came to the rescue of my ass and saved it with a fast lie. It started with a father's son in need of a haircut one Saturday morning at the Institute. A simple all over clipper cut with a number four guard, followed up with a straight clipper for the ears and neckline. Any stay at home mom could have performed this piece of work blindfolded with ease. It was a piece of cake, a no-brainer, which would grant me a fast cup of coffee and a much needed cigarette break and perhaps even a tip before lunch.

I seated this young man at my station and with the shake and pop of a fresh cutting cape, he was ready for service. Following his father's instructions to the 'T', with my clipper in hand I proceeded buzzing smoothly over his head with the finesse and style of a salon star in the making. The kid had a small head and I was finished in about five minutes or less. Then I removed the number four guard from the head of my clipper and while I was making quick work of his sideburns and neckline I noticed a few small hairs on top of his head I had missed. "An easy fix" I thought. With a fast swipe of the clipper they were gone and so was a two inch by three inch square patch of hair from the scalp of his head In my haste I had forgotten to reattach the number four guard to the blade of my clipper. It was the "Oh shit " moment of all time and right now it was all mine. Everything just stopped. As far as I was concerned, any debt that I ever owed to the universe was now paid in full. What I had to do now was above and beyond the call of duty for a hairdresser. I had to man up fast before presenting this unfortunate situation to a father in waiting.

There was no way in hell to remedy this screw up because there was no such thing as a fake hair, fast patch, super glue repair kit for idiots. My only hope was that cool heads would prevail. I made my way to the waiting area feeling like a surgeon about to share the worst news possible for a parent concerning a child. I've had a lot of practice with talking myself out of some tense situations and it was a good thing I had improved at it. If there was ever a time for a gold halo wrapped lie, it was now!

"Sir, there was an unfortunate situation that occurred while performing your son's haircut. Would you please come with me." Together his Father and I made our way back to my station.

With his Dad now eyeballing the bald square patch atop his son's head he was experiencing an unfortunate moment of his own. Then he asked in a slow, deep voice "What happened?"

"Sir, I'm sorry, but it was a situation beyond my control that occurred. The clipper guard just fell off the blade as I was finishing your son's haircut." The kid and his father were fairly good sports about this act of fate. It was like a zen experience for the three of us that was taking place.

He asked slowly "Is there anything you can do?"

"Yes Sir, there is. I can shave the rest of his head to match."

"No thank you. That won't be necessary. Just take off the cape please. Son, let's go home...your Mom's gonna freak and then she's gonna go ape. "

"I'm very sorry Sir for this unfortunate accident."

His father said nothing and while holding his son's hand they just walked away. That was it. Can you believe an instructor never found out? Since the universe was clearly aware of my senseless act of negligence regarding my client's haircut, I felt no need to inform an instructor. I knew the universe would deal with this situation at another time so why should I add a pen whipping that wasn't needed to my student file? When I was asked where my client was, I just said "I don't know, they just got up and left " What amazed me about all of this was that nobody weirded out and went off when they had every right to do so. This could have gone the other way and turned out to be a really bad scene. That kid must have known my ass was on the line because he never once said shit about what really happened. I've often thought of him as my angel from heaven who never ratted me out during my moment from hell.

I was lucky because this situation could have resulted in a dismissal from the Institute. Behind closed doors, Horst would have been rolling on his ass in laughter as he wrote a letter of condolence to the Veterans Administration for the loss of a student due to a careless act of professional negligence, which could have severely damaged the reputation of the Institute and it's staff. Fortunately for me, that didn't happen. Being clever, crafty, and lucky were the things that contributed to my success as a student when I needed them most.

My first year at the Institute has almost ended and so has the cold winter of '88. The heat wave we experienced over the summer, with it's humidity and drought, was as uncomfortable physically as the winter had been before it. Kara and I had ended our relationship on a good note. We were able to do this because we were friends and cared about each other but what I missed the most was that we never played together again. We would still shoot the shit over a cup of coffee now and then, but it just wasn't what it had once been.

On the outside I was looking good but on the inside I felt ugly as hell. We've all been left on the side of the road holding our hats in our hands but why does it always seem like your ex finds somebody else first?

Sometimes less is more, and now that Kara and I were no longer hanging out and swapping spit freed up my social calendar. I made good use of this time by reading one self help book after another. There was no getting around it. I had become a therapy junkie in need of a quick fix that would comfort the pain of my bruised ego. It was a sad scene to know my love life was back on the shelf again as a returned item. Love always has a blessing, and sometimes it's the absence of the one we once valued more so than the company we once kept.

Kara had graduated and was no longer at the Institute. She lucked out with a position with Horst at his Spa Reserve in Wisconsin. I was happy to hear she landed that gig. She was happy about it because she had plenty of friends from the Institute to work with at the Reserve. That girl had a good head on her shoulders and it wouldn't surprise me one bit if she wasn't running that place in six months or so. It would be nice to run into that rascal again someday just to find out whatever became of her.

The few ladies I hung out with before attending the Institute were from my neighborhood of West Baltimore. Most of us had grown up together and they knew me well before and after I returned from Vietnam. Many of the neighborhood girls worked at the open market on Hollins Street. Often they were affectionately referred to as the 'Market Wenches' of West Baltimore. Those of us who were locals, and known, could get away with shouting out such a handle but I wouldn't recommend it for a stranger passing by to ever consider using it. The market was open for business Thursday, Friday and Saturday, three days a week and twelve hours a day. Unloading, lifting and carrying heavy crates of fruits and vegetables was some damn hard work, especially in the heat and humidity of a Maryland summer. If you were from the neighborhood and the stall owners knew you, they took care of you well. You may have worked for 36 hours but they would pay you for 40 and every week you had 4 days off. That was like a mini vacation once a week with a day left to rest up before returning to work.

The resort town of Ocean City was a three hour drive south of Baltimore. The hotel rates during the week were much cheaper than over the weekends. On Mondays, Tuesdays and Wednesdays of any late spring, summer or early fall you would find our 'Market Wenches' sunning themselves on the beaches during the day and cooling off at the resort's hot spots during the night. Their whole thing was beer, having fun and getting rowdy together. The hard work of the market toned their bodies well and the sun's rays on the beach made them glow with a natural beauty. The lot of these lasses never went to college, or even a trade school for that matter, but they were street smart and nobody's fool. These sweethearts were born and bred Micks from the neighborhood. They were lovely and of strong character and deserving of respect. If you were dating one, she would stand by you no matter what and cover your back in a bar fight as well. But if she ever caught you lying or cheating on her, you could find yourself in a world of hurt. That was the wrong way to cross the line in a big way that left no way to peddle back because her reputation was now on the line. This could get your ass rat packed in an instant. After they chewed you up and spit you out, there wouldn't be enough of you left that a cannibal could find to make soup out of your bones.

Sometimes love affairs have a way of removing us from the closeness of our friends, especially us guys. We'll give up our sports and our buddies in less time than it takes to say a fast "See you later" just to hang out with a hot babe. I don't need a high five on that because we all know it's true. Men are shameless. If we're not thinking with our dicks we're acting on their behalf. I am not trying to suggest that we're not without loyalty to our friends because we are. When things fall out with our gals, we fall back in with our pals, ASAP.

Somehow all that changed after I started beauty school. The Institute was a very health conscious environment that could contribute to the rebirth of just about anything or anybody. It only stands to reason that the healthier we became mentally and physically would in turn attract healthier relationships in our lives.

Every once in a while, I would score with some rich guy's girlfriend or trophy wife. Quality time with one of these ladies wasn't such a hard thing to find if you were witty with words and knew how to read between their lines. Their flirty small talk was nothing more than to determine if you were a potential fuck buddy or not. These ladies had a sensual courage when they saw something or somebody they wanted and like an aroused cat, they were ready to play. The trick was you had to know how to recognize it from the start. If they sensed neediness you were out because they had plenty of that at home.

Sometimes just the way they touched your hand or forearm in passing to say hello was enough to let you know there was interest here, if you wanted it. Their power was in their smile, that's why they used it to greet the world. That brief moment of eye contact you just shared was used like a tractor beam to suck you in. Most of these ladies were married to squares and stiffs to begin with, but the size and depth of their wealth and power mattered. Crossing the line every once in a while with a boy toy from the Institute was a refreshing change from the same old thing at home. This was to become my introduction into the politics of the beauty industry.

When it came to the professional needs of my clients, I was always on task. Soon I learned that who you were doing was just as important as what you were doing for the needs of your clients and your career. How do you think Jon Peters went from hairdresser to film director and producer? Giving Barbra the look of an afro head job wasn't the only thing he could perform skillfully.

If a trophy wife should ever ask "Do you work with men's hair?" By all means say no. The last thing you want are their husbands for clients. Family affairs are not what you want in your chairs. The thing about a trophy wife was you never knew when she was going to show up. She could surprise the hell out of you, dropping by at school when you least expected it. Another thing was the late night phone call at home with an invite for a glass of wine if you were up for it. I often wondered why many of them never suffered from Acute Anxiety Disorder and then I figured it out. It was because they were loving every minute of it. These gals did a lot of therapeutic activities such as shopping a.k.a. retail therapy. It was always available and the added plus was that it was cheaper than psychiatry.

Sometimes you can win a heart with something handmade, like a haircut for instance. No wonder our clients love us so much. A blonde Norwegian by the name of Janet was one such person in my life during my time at the Institute. She had it all - A great job as a buyer for a large corporation, paying serious cash and lots of travel. She was the bread winner in her family and she knew that she was putting in more than she was getting out. The only thing that stopped her from moving out was the love she had for her children and the fact that her parents simply adored her husband. She was afraid of hurting the people she loved the most, so she chose to stay married and live a double life. Janet was well disciplined with the limits and boundaries she had set for her life. Even as an adulteress spouse she was able to create a morality she could coexist with responsibly.

There was a lot of interest and chemistry shared between Janet and myself. The affair for her and I wasn't one of a sexual nature, but that of a very emotional one. Whenever I heard from her it always felt like she was taking a shot in the dark when calling me. We could only spend an hour or two together, at the most, because she never wanted to create any suspicions for her husband at home. Whenever we hooked up at a café or bar, it was always good and a time out for both of us from the rest of the world. No matter how much time passed between us we were always able to pick up where we had left off. We were two people that were very attracted to each other but the bonds of blood proved to be stronger than those of water. Every once in a while I hear an old song by Steely Dan titled "Dirty Work" and I think of us. I hope in some way I was able to help her remember how she used to feel and how she used to be. Everybody deserves to be happy.

Next week was graduation for the class of '88 and even Lenny's class pets, the poster children of gay pride, made it through with the rest of us. Smokin' hairstyle? Check. New shoes with killer heels? Check. No junk in the trunk? Check. When everything was checking these rookies were feeling fabulous. They knew business and social options would soon beckon and they were out to turn heads.

Most of the new talents would be going out into the industry seeking fame and fortune. Who knows? Maybe a job in Hollywood as a hairdresser to the stars or, perhaps, staying here and working for Mister Big himself. I just hope they're knowing where they're going, with a plan that works after they get there. Sometimes even our best efforts don't always pay off. As for me, sometimes I just can't get enough of a good thing. I decided to stay on another year and complete the next program of Esthiology here at the Institute. Everybody's packing up and getting ready to leave town but ain't nobody going no place until they settle up with those student loans first.

Some bureaucrat once said that the only sure things in life are death and taxes. He must not have gotten past high school or else he would have included the shady shakedowns of student loans. Neediness has a scent about itself and predatory lenders are always searching for the prospects of the poor to feed upon. Student loans are the first and last order of business here at the Institute, and most schools in general. As students, we live or die by the acceptance or denials of our school loans and grants.

Why does it cost so much bread to attend a beauty school when the clients are paying for the services in the first place? Every month when I make a payment on my student loan I check the small print on the billing statement. It makes me feel like the sucker of a lost soul who has signed a deal with the devil. Then I eyeball the envelope just to see if it was postmarked in hell.

During the Vietnam War a lot of college grads made their way to Canada to avoid the draft. That was a bunch of bullshit. The truth was, they split town to get out of repaying their student loans. All I can say is "Good for you and smart thinking on your part". To use the war was a great excuse and a quick fix for your self image as well. How it went down with the credit bureau was an added bonus. It was entered on your credit history that you were a conscientious objector instead of a deadbeat credit risk. Let's not make an enemy out of the essential. I know it's a major cold cocker but we have to pay to play so let's embrace it as an ally and move on. I shouldn't gripe so much because I've got it a lot better than most. Besides, it's worth every dime it costs to attend the Horst Institute because of the old man's name on it alone.

I'm still cutting heads at The Bootleg Salon in the Frat Shack. Uncle Sam's dead presidents have shown up when they were needed most and secured a treaty with the shylocks of my school loans. I'm still reading tarot cards to cover the extras I need to live the life of a responsible student heathen in the style that I have now become accustomed to.

Some of the students here are so deep in hock it must feel like a pawn shop instead of a school. Everybody knows the IRS are a bunch of dicks when it comes to collecting back taxes and are hell bent on getting paid. The collection agencies for delinquent school loans are bigger dicks yet. Cheat creeps beware. These guys will come after you with the vengeance of a pissed off bail bondsman that you skipped town on. If you owe them money make a deal or, in some cases, make a new deal and pay up. Don't try cockfighting with these guys because you will lose and your reputation will be damaged as well. The hell of a student loan is awaiting the promise of a future heaven that only comes after it is rubber stamped in red and marked...PAID IN FULL.

All I can say is that I am having the best time of my life here at the Institute while living with a house full of friends at the Frat Shack and with all the beer and pizzas we bounce checks for, every meal's a feast.

I never suffered from reclusive anxiety, nor the depression of cabin fever while living here at the Frat Shack. Why? Because our student life style was the antidote for the emotional chills of a long and cloudy winter. A party on most weekends was how we got around it. I don't recall one case of Seasonal Affective Disorder in the Frat Shack the entire time I lived there. I've always thought of myself as a southern boy and I've never cared much for the idea of becoming a snow vulture in disguise.

Sunday mornings were always my sought after hours for sleeping in. I guess it was because I found them quiet and peaceful after a Saturday night out on the town. During the school week it's not always this tranquil around here but it was today and God knows I needed it. The hour on the face of my jack hammer clock was showing 11:00 a.m. - Wow! Why does a hangover always show up with a bad taste in your mouth first? No matter how often it happens, it's just something you never get used to. I guess it's a good example of what happens when things return to their source.

Besides some coffee and a cigarette, there was an added bonus for this morning of comfort. It was the end of the school year and nobody was leaving town without some play time in the streets first. The campus had become a cosmic osmosis. No one gave a shit about the juicy gossip making its way back and biting them in the ass because nobody was going to be around to hear about it. Dinkytown, a.k.a. the Hell's Kitchen rip off of Minneapolis, would soon be full of bar hopping jocks, babes in wet t-shirts, and dorm party keggers.

For the Frats on Fraternity Row it was just like Mardi Gras in the Big Easy. This wasn't just another day and no way in hell was it going to become just an ordinary night. The Frat boys were on scavenger hunts and everything from the zombie pub crawlers to the voodoo queens of Goth-mania were considered fair game for the taking. A few old cougars were also on the prowl, hoping to make fast work of the young and healthy, who were often the lame and needy with the thirst and curiosity of a first timer. The key for having a good time was showing your true colors and letting your freak flag fly. Those were the rules of the game that made you a player.

Tonight was a reward for the things that had been done well and the memories of our times together well spent. Soon the guys and gals of summer would be gone. Some I would see again and others probably not. Before long, Dinkytown would take on the look of a deserted mining camp whose wealth had panned out. In the fall of the year hundreds of new settlers would pour into town once more and again, the gold rush for the credit cards and the greenbacks would be on.

The Frat Shack was now empty except for Randy, Arthur and myself. Randy would be spending a brief time with his family on vacation in Boston. Arthur was soon on his way back to New Mexico. As for me, I'm a gypsy by nature and as lucky as lucky can be. I landed a position as an assistant for an old money salon in Mt. Washington, just outside of Baltimore, Maryland. It's funny how matters of design can bring people together. Sometimes an act of chance can unleash a whole new range of possibilities if one is willing to step out and test the waters.

One thing for sure, everybody was going to split somewhere for the summer. For some, it was the comfort of home once more after the first time of being away for so long. The diehard party hounds were in Amsterdam smoking the best the bars had to offer and afterwards window shopping the eye candy of the Red Light Square. Most of the jocks ended up at beach resorts as lifeguards during the day and bouncers for the clubs at night. The geeks went backpacking, wherever geeks go backpacking and I had no idea of where that place was. What I wanted to know was how in the hell did they ever find their way back to us again?

Jock or geek, homeboy or chick, everybody had one thing in common about leaving town, and that was all the useless shit they left behind. The amount of work needed for an end of year school clean up was unbelievable. It was just one of those things that you couldn't put off when it was your job to get it done and you were the one who had to do it. Thank goodness, Randy and Arthur stuck around another day and helped me out. This must have been one of the times Winston Churchill was talking about when he said "Never have so few done so much for so many". After viewing what resembled a communal garbage heap, the words of Karl Marx now entered my mind. "To each according to his abilities and to each according to his needs". I felt screwed by both.

The Frat Shack looked the same to me now as the first day I had seen it over a year ago. I didn't mind cleaning the place up now because there was a face, name and story behind every cup, can and bottle I picked up. Some had become the best of friends and others could be real "mofos" at times. Some of each would be returning in September. Cleaning the Frat Shack was just another way of earning my keep around here. The 50-percent rent reduction was still a gift from heaven Randy had given me for services rendered that had covered my butt way back in the beginning. By the end of the following day my work was done and once again the house gleamed with the gloss of a spit shine I had given it with the care of my touch.

The house was safe and secure now as I left and locked the door behind me. Before leaving, I looked at the Mezuzah on the frame of the doorway entrance. I kissed it with my two fingers and thanked God for the kindness and good deeds that were given to me during my stay in the house of his Chosen People.

The need to create and contribute
an object of lasting worth
that could make a difference
has always been the source of my salvation.

Many times I've failed, in spite of my best efforts,
until the force of my will
provided me with the ability
to pursue the needs of my desires.

Chapter 12: Callings

After graduation I finally made my way back to Baltimore. It was a long drive home, but it was there I began and there I am happiest. One thing for sure about East Coast folks, we do love our seafood and I was looking forward to some Maryland crab cakes and cold beer real soon.

I've been gone just over a year and I was thinking how good it was going to feel just to eat and sleep in my sister's home again. Our family members had passed long ago and even though they were gone, there were plenty of pictures that reminded me of our times shared as a family.

When it comes to relationships all we can do is enjoy the ride, bumps and all. Old places and old faces are always good to see because, once again, we can touch and feel our roots. My life long friend, Greg Senkus, and I would be doing some catching up while hanging out at some of our favorite bars down in Fells Point near the Inner Harbor.

Besides family, friends and beer joints, there was another thing waiting here in town - a job. Before coming home for the summer I had contacted the owner of a salon known as Pat's Place for Hair. After a few phone conversations with the owner, I had a good feeling about it working out very well. The salon was located in the center of Mt. Washington, just outside of Baltimore and very close to my sister's house.

Pat did a good job over the phone and was very thorough in describing the personality and the atmosphere of his salon and the clientele of the community it served. This place turned out to be everything he said it was and then some.

Pat had lived in Austria for many years and he was fluent in French and German. He wanted to offer something different for the clients of his salon that no other salon was giving and that was the touch and style that only a European salon could provide. It was right here, in a small town, that a lot of wealthy people called home. He was business savvy and knew he had made a good environmental and financial decision to settle here.

I was a graduate of the Horst Institute and having me around for the summer as a salon assistant was a good thing for the shop and for me as well. This was a great place to keep your eyes peeled for some lucky opportunities to work and learn from some very talented artists. The clientele of the salon were mainly the relatives and friends of old money families that had lived in this community for generations. Quite a few of them held high positions on Capitol Hill in Washington, DC. It wasn't unusual at all for politics to be discussed over a glass of wine while a stylist and an assistant attended to the needs of their hair.

The town had the quaint look of a Christmas card. It was full of small shops, pubs and sidewalk cafés. The cobblestone streets and brick sidewalks, with their gas burning lamps at every corner, only added to the charm and character of this lovely place. I was captured by it the moment I arrived, and someday I hope to return as a resident. I had sent a good resumé and laid out my best bullshit over the phone during our conversations regarding my position as an assistant for his salon. The truth is, it was the reputation of the Horst Institute that got my foot through the front door of Pat's salon. I was a student from the finest school in the country for hair design and the old man's name was my calling card.

I knew there were going to be expectations and I was hell bent on achieving them. My interview with Pat went very well. This may have been the place he ended up at, but I could tell it wasn't the kind of place he started out from. Just like me, he had made it here from the streets but before reaching the streets, he had to fight his way out of the alleys. He was a man of moral stature and wouldn't hesitate to take off his coat and start popping his knuckles with anybody who wasn't. His questions to me were straight and to the point and that was the way I answered him back. In no way was I going to try spoonfeeding this man with what I thought he wanted to hear. I knew when to listen to what he had to say and I knew when to shut up. He leaned back in his chair with his hands clasped and his index fingers pointing toward his chin. Pat wasn't thinking with his head, he was feeling with his gut. After a few moments of silent contemplation he gave me a half smile, stood up, shook my hand and welcomed me to his salon.

I was to be his personal assistant, first and foremost, for the needs of his clients. I greeted and prepared the clients for the service of other stylists as well, when Pat permitted me to do so. Pat was a fair and honest man. He was the lead dog of the shop and had no problem showing some teeth, if need be.

Pat performed his craft with the grace and style of a nobleman's heart joyfully beating with a dancer's rhythm. His attention to detail was executed as though he possessed the eye of a cinematographer doing a closeup of a style's shape and movement. One day while working with a client together, Pat asked me "Joseph, how do you make perfect curls?"

I answered back "By making perfect circles!"

He smiled while nodding his head and looking around the salon. Returning his attention to me, in a relaxed tone, he said "Joseph, would you mind serving our guest some wine?"

"I would be happy to. I'll take care of it right away."

Pat wasn't asking me to be a waiter but he knew I would approach his clients in a manner that reflected the professionalism and ambience of his salon. This was a recognition of his trust and confidence in me as his personal assistant. Here at Pat's Place it was all about respect, and the needs and cares of the clients always came first.

The small town of Mt. Washington was a beautiful place to visit and with it's proximity to Baltimore, it was an ideal place to live and set up a shop. Pat's Place was known for the excellence of it's services and for the old money clientele that frequented his salon.

Old money clients are a breed of their own and they took some time getting used to, especially for an outsider like me, to become comfortable working with them. One of the quirky things about these clients was understanding how they mentally processed stuff in their heads. They're always so cool, calm and collected about anything that needs to be dealt with at any given moment. There was no such thing as a bad hair day - it was good hat day! With these Blue Bloods perception was like a top and they knew how to put a spin on it. You never know what they're thinking, even when on the inside they're reacting and going off the frigging map about it.

Every once in a while they would become easily annoyed whenever they saw one of the nuevo rich taking advantage of their wealth and exploiting the less fortunate. In many ways, the true Blue Bloods were champions for the underdog as long as you were not trying to marry into their family and create a litter with one of their bitches. That was a social no, no! They often conveyed both a feeling of great wealth, ease and comfort. Never mistake this lot for a lack of back bone, in spite of their congeniality and good nature. If need be, they could become very proficient in the art of using their wit and intellect as a weapon. They may have been warm, generous and kindly, but they're used to people doing what they say and having their own way. Money was thought of as a tool for success but more so as family property, which was well managed and maintained.

Buyers remorse was unheard of with this clan. Their accumulation of wealth was the result of sound reason and strategic planning because they believed in protecting the things that mattered. A family's legacy was measured by the accumulation of wealth and property, passed on from one generation to the next like the genetic code of their ancestry. For me, Pat's salon was like attending a charm school for the nobles of the hairdressing industry and getting paid for it while I was there.

In the beauty industry all eyes and ears were on the Horst Institute and the Aveda hair care product line. Aveda products were now in the process of going international. The bar had been raised to the next level and Aveda was it. To have a student from the Institute as an assistant in your salon was considered fortunate and desirable. We were a sought after item of the time and I enjoyed being on the bubble. Our students were formally educated in the format of European hair design and had a strong background knowledge of the Aveda product line. Having one of us in your salon was like having your own on site educator and product knowledge advisor as well. This is what I was bringing to the table and Pat was as happy as hell about it. Any success I helped create for his salon and staff would continue, no matter if I stayed or moved on, so having me around for a few months was a no-brainer situation for all.

On the outside, the stylists for the entitled, the rich and the famous were much like the clients they serviced. A public display of proper behavior and professional ethics was a must. Most of the time the break room was a place for coffee, cigarettes and conversations full of a weeks worth of shop gossip. Of course, we blabbed about our clients behind their backs telling one secret after another. We couldn't help ourselves - some of their shit was so good that it just needed to be put out there.

Creative people tend to wear their feelings on their sleeves and that can be dangerous because every once in a while that green dragon, known as jealousy, will fire up and show itself. In this business, no matter how smart or creative you are, you can still get hurt and some of these pains can take a long time to heal. At times, I couldn't believe how a staff of professional adults could behave like a bunch of pissed off schoolgirls. Sometimes, it was like watching cats and pit bulls having a go at it and making a hell of a lot out of a hell of a little. Why so many people get so worked up over nothing is beyond me. I must have been born with a special gene that kept me calm in the face of this kind of egotistical drama. I wished I could spread it around a little because I think a few of the creative hearts around here could've used it.

Every hairdresser in the business knows there are two rules of the game we play by. Number one is that hairdressers lose clients and rule number two is that hairdressers can't change rule number one. It's never good for the ego when a stylist loses a high profile client to another salon, but it does happen. It's not a question of if, but when? There's only one thing worse. When you start losing your clients to a coworker in your own salon, then it becomes a real tear jerking scene.

This is the kiss of death for the ego that is beyond healing, for most. My best advice is to always be on the lookout for new clients. Keep a list of new prospects for the future no matter how booked you become. Never take your clients for granted and always be willing to give that extra touch for the ones you have. They give us their heads and are rooting for us to do something spectacular with them besides a little off the top, close around the ears and square up the back. People, by nature, are social animals and nothing satisfies and excites us more than a wide variety of creature features. It can be an emotionally frustrating experience when this part of our physiology is screaming out for some TLC and professional attention. When you fail to return the favor, your clients will find somebody who will.

My professional life at the salon was very rewarding but my social life was in need of a romantic hookup. While attending the Institute and residing in the Frat Shack, my love life was often full of the self centered shenanigans of a school boy gone wild. I was a mess and the girls I went out with were also a mess so we ended up becoming a mess together. If I wasn't with a two sided gal like Kara, I was shoplifting the booty of somebody else's stock. I was used to falling for the first girl that gave me some attention because I was afraid of being alone.

I believe my job here at the salon, with it's protocol and responsibilities, may have served as a shock treatment that guided and matured me far beyond my wayward past. Sometimes the need for love can turn fantasies into a reality. When you're new in town and a bit lonely, working in a beauty salon might just be the right place to ignite some fireworks to light up your life. My eye for design has grown a bit keener these days, especially for the movement and style of a classic shape like the one who just stepped through the salon door. She was in need of a haircut but didn't have an appointment and soon I would know her name was Lorie. The salon was busy as hell and no one was taking another client that day, much less a new one without an appointment. Our receptionist wasn't about to let money just walk out the door unhappy. She politely said to our lady in need that we have a salon assistant available and would that suit her needs?

Unaware of what a salon assistant was, Lorie said "Sure, that would be fine."

Our receptionist informed me of a client needing a cut and asked if I was available to accommodate her. As fate would have it, Pat had left the salon early that day and without his clients to assist I needed something to do. Our receptionist introduced us and I escorted Lorie to my station. Our design consultation wasn't much of a big deal so I made up for it with a very relaxing shampoo and scalp massage with a conditioning treatment.

Lorie was open and friendly from the moment we met and she knew how to put a smile out there that could lift a guy off his feet. Seeing her for the first time in my life felt like meeting a blind date that I clicked with and couldn't wait to know more about. Working with her hair felt more like having a good time with a close friend than performing a service on a paying customer. Her cut was very easy to do. It was a bob with an undercut around the perimeter. Styled with a round brush and a blow dryer, she could have been good to go in less than an hour but I was enjoying my time with her so why rush a good thing. I decided to milk this for a while just to see what might become of it. The lip service between her and I wasn't the usual small talk that goes back and forth between a client and a stylist. This felt more open and personal, even a tad bit arousing in a comfortable way.

She asked if I was new in town. I said no and that I had family here, but I was living in Minneapolis as a student and was here as a salon assistant for the summer. She looked at me with that smile again and said "So, you're a school boy, huh?"

"Yeah, I guess you could say that but I'm definitely more of a senior than a freshman."

Just before leaving, she wrote down her number and said if I was interested in checking out some of the night life in Baltimore, just give her a call. Sparing all the details, this is how I met Lorie.

We spent a lot of time together that summer in Baltimore. The Inner Harbor was one of our favorite places to walk around after a night of hanging out at Hammer Jacks Saloon. There was so much to see here and enjoy on a beautiful summer night. The brightly colored neon lights reflecting off the water from the restaurants, bars and hotels created an inviting sight to behold. A romantic ride around the harbor in a water taxi, with the sound and smell of the sea close by, made for the end of a perfect evening.

Lorie was a sales executive and the go to person for commercial advertising time with the broadcast studio here in Baltimore. She was smart, rich and beautiful. She wasn't at all the kind of girl I had been used to. There was something about her I had never seen before and it was everything I ever wanted. A Zen proverb says that when the disciple is ready, the teacher appears. Lorie showed me how far I had come, and the place I was at now was worth every challenge I had faced along the way of my journey. Because of her I learned what, mattered was that in spite of all the things I had been through, I had survived and I was alive.

Summer would soon be over and shortly I would be returning to the Institute and the city of Minneapolis. The town of Mt. Washington, it's people and the staff of Pat's Place had been wonderful to me. It had been a good time, with plenty of warm memories to tide me over for another cold winter in Minnesota. Before I knew it, I was back at the Frat Shack and attending the Institute in less than a week after I had left Baltimore. Not much had changed here except for the arrival of a few new faces. The life style was the same and so were the times on Fraternity Row.

It was good to see Randy again and renew old friendships at school and in the house. When I returned, I discovered my jackhammer clock had been busted all to hell. That pissed me off. I knew my clock could be a pain in the ass but it was my pain in the ass and no one had the right to bang it up. That clock had served me well so many times, getting people up and out the door when I needed them to leave. Randy had rented out my room and the use of my clock over the summer while I was gone. My guess is the clock must have scared the hell out of some renter one morning and that's how it ended up against the wall.

At first, it felt a little strange returning to the Institute and living in the Frat Shack again. The fact that my clock was history only added to the uneasiness I felt now. I think I may have returned to my home away from home with a slight touch of homesickness. My body may have been here in Minneapolis but my thoughts and feelings were still back in Baltimore. I was stressed out over being here when I wanted to be there with Lorie. It felt like a split that was tearing me apart. Calling her would have only made things worse - she was there and I was here and that was it.

Soon I was excited again by the atmosphere of Fraternity Row and seeing old faces did me good. By the end of the month I was right back in the groove again. I regarded it as just one of those things that happens between friends - no matter how much time passes between us, we always manage to hit it off again. Who knows? Maybe lightning would strike twice for Lorie and I again someday.

Since I've known both sides of the fence now, I can honestly say that life as an Esthiology student was a piece of cake compared to that of a hair design grunt. For me, the peace and tranquility of the Esthiology Clinic was much more relaxed. There just seemed to be less chi-chi nonsense and drama in this crowd than I experienced while in the hair design unit.

The study of Esthiology is the science of skin care, it's anatomy and biology. Another part of this study was the health care and maintenance regime provided by the Aveda skin care product line. The state of the art product line of Aveda contributed immensely to the appearance of the skin and the longevity of it's beauty. All students here at the Institute, no matter what program of choice they pursued, had a strong background knowledge of all the Aveda hair and skin care products.

The artistry of Esthiology included the various cosmetic and statement application techniques. Last but not least, were those relaxation pleasures of a daily facial massage. These practice sessions were always performed in the morning hours before taking clients during the afternoon. What a way to start the day when we needed it the most.

The downside for me was making sure I shaved extra close every morning and removed any nasal hair that may have been showing. I wouldn't have wanted another student to feel disgusted about anything that was growing out of my nose. In those situations, they saw everything they needed to see about you and the use of small talk was futile. There just wasn't going to be any eye contact or lip service shared. Not that this has ever happened to me, but I've heard my share of stories from those that it had. I've spent more time in rehabilitation centers than most drug dealers and bank robbers have done hitches in prison. Healing is one of our salvations and I envy those that can help others along the way. Why is it that those who are seeking so much purity for the world create so much shit that the rest of us have to live with? Some deal well with suffering, while others simply stand by and watch.

For a Nam Vet coming here, just out of a Rehab Center with a helluva little, I would soon be leaving with a helluva lot. The additional time and money I spent here at the Institute turned out to be a wise move on my part. For the first time in my life I saw nothing wrong with investing in myself. I not only added another marketable skill to my talent as a hairdresser but somehow life here had unfolded perfectly for me as well. My eight block walk, via the Arctic Circle of Dinkytown, had not changed during the cold mornings of another winter and the warmth of friendship always awaited me at Jim's Café. My life as a student at the Institute and a resident of the Frat Shack had been damn good for me.

The house had gone co-ed at the beginning of the school year and we had a new resident that was a single mom who was attending the U of M. Randy and I both agreed that she needed a break that would help her make ends meet while attending school. We decided to let her live in the house, with her son, during the school year for free. Her name was Mary and her son's name was Matt - cute kid. She did a great job of keeping the house clean and it made her happy to know that she was earning her keep. Matt and his mother were deserted, with no means of support, by the one person they depended on the most, his father. Falling on hard times was usually the response of abandonment for a single mom and a fatherless child. They had become the product of an environment that wasn't their fault, but they had to live with it as though it was. Something told me that everything would work out okay for Mary and Matt someday down the road, as it had for me.

Every year it's the same, and it's been happening as long as landlords and property service agencies can remember. Loads of garbage, tables, lamps, carpet, clothes, chairs, shoes, books, broken mirrors, couches, futons and more futons are the remains of the moving process that lay on the front and back lawns of the Frat Houses on Fraternity Row. One of my very best friends to this day, Randy, would be staying at the house for another two years. With renting rooms to students and renting the party room to Frats, the house had become a fat, cash cow that he wasn't ready to part with. Everybody's waiting for their boat to come in and mine showed up the day I arrived here, over two years ago, and now I was ready to go home. I finished up school here in June of 1990 and somehow I managed completing all three programs at the Institute. I left school with three diplomas that reflected the places I had been and were the treasures of my memories while there. The day I graduated, I found myself outside the Institute now as a bystander and no longer the student of a great school. Soon it would be time to pack up and begin a new life. I felt like a bird ready to leave the nest and it was now up to me to prove that I could fly. Horst noticed me standing there as he was crossing the street to enter the Institute. He walked up, shook my hand and asked if I would do one more thing for him someday.

"Sure Horst, what would that be?"

He whispered in my ear "Joseph, I want you to stop smoking for me."

Well, those weren't the words I was expecting to hear at such a moment - a personal mantra perhaps for my ears only or at least something a little less generic. Horst, if you ever read this book...I want you to know that I eventually quit smoking and it was the hardest thing I have ever done. As far as I am concerned, you owe me one.

I can't believe what learning how to use a comb, scissors and a blow dryer has done for my life. The call of my shears brought me out of the confines of a Rehab unit at a Veterans Medical Center. They have carved a place for me in the mainstream of society. No doubt, they are my most valued possessions. I would never consider parting ways with them for even a moment. Since the day the comb was created, a curiosity and mind set born of nonsense and exaggerations have floated around this art like a phantom. The mystique of a hairdresser is often prevalent in the minds of the clients we serve, yet they share the personal secrets of their lives frequently because we become their Father confessor. We give them an ear while we adorn their crowns with the touch of our hands. My guess is, this trend will continue long into the future because it has survived most of our past. The ego of a human being often catches a bad rap in our society but in our business the ego is our best client and we love that rascal, BIG TIME. Where would we be without it? Our job is easily defined. We're here to help people look HOT!

Somebody said that clothes make the woman and the man. As a hairdresser, I say bullshit. Only hair can change the appearance of both. A skilled hairdresser can improve the features of a client's face in an instant. The personality can become more upbeat as well because when we look good, we feel good. CLOTHES CAN'T DO THAT.

I believe becoming a hairdresser and a massage therapist restored a sense of proportion and balance into my life once more. Some of us are luckier or more successful than others. Who knows? Perhaps one of the superstars of our industry will become immortalized someday. I can see it now, Horst Rechelbacher captured as a wax figure in the Smithsonian. His eternal pose - cutting and blow drying the head of a mannequin, behind the length of a velvet rope.

It is not my intention to imply that Horst may have invented hair. I can, however, credit him with creating an Institute in the United States where his students would become hairdressers known around the world as true artists and professionals. He revolutionized and reinvented the technical and creative theme of modern day hair design, while preserving the classical history of it's past. If a man's work can bridge the gap between life and death, and if it can live on long after he has died as an object of worth, then he has achieved his greatest success.

I, for one, believe that Horst has attained his immortality.

I have long since retired from
this business of hair.

I have traded the feel of the
scissor for the touch of a pen.

But as long as I live,
I will never forget the hold of
a rifle and the sight of
a fixed bayonet.

People ask if I brought any
souvenirs from Vietnam.
I answer them "Yeah, Me."

Joseph Ross

JANE FONDA
AMERICAN TRAITOR
BITCH

Afterward

T here's nothing like the confidence and satisfaction you get from knowing you saw something through to the very end. My stories are truthful but yet, I'm always getting a lot of incredulous looks in response to them. I can't help it if my life is more colorful, interesting and complex than the movies. I can't think of a better place for this initial paragraph than here at the very beginning of the afterward. I can't remember, did I mention a roller coaster ride at the beginning of this book? I remember saying we were going out there for a real ride, but I forgot to mention the ups and downs of an emotional roller coaster that would leave us feeling a bit bipolar when it was over. All kidding aside, I think we had a pretty good run together during the course of our journey.

I hope that sharing my life with you through this book has touched your spirit and enhanced your experience as a human being. My path in life is just one example of the human condition in action among the billions that take place every single, solitary day. Hannibal Lecter said "We covet the things we see every day". I hope you've experienced enough with me that will inspire your reflections again and again.

Besides my wife Nancy being the love of my life and the best deal I ever made, I have something else on the side that I run around with. She's a Softail. Her road name is Cracker, she looks like a Night Train and she comes from a place known as Harley Davidson. I guess you can tell from my general attitude that I'm not the type who can sit around very well.

Human nature exhibits the aspects of eternity and infinity

(endless space and time), but for human beings, our biological clocks are ticking. For Vietnam Veterans our time hasn't run out, but it is running thin. In case you haven't been paying attention over the last few decades since the Vietnam War ended, the clock for Vietnam Veterans has been ticking a lot faster than for the Veterans of other Wars.

Some of these statistics were very depressing for me at first, but in another sense I felt a great deal of pride. Of the 2,709,918 Americans who served in Vietnam, less than 850,000 are estimated to be alive today. The youngest American Vietnam Veterans would be approximately 55 - 56 years of age. Since I am still alive today, I feel honored to be among the last. Most Americans out here don't have a clue about this, and sadly neither do many Nam Vets as well. When I discovered this, it gave me the chills. This is the kind of news that most of us are used to reading about for our World War II and Korean War Veterans. In the last 14 years we have been dying too fast, and if the rate continues, only a few of us will survive by the year 2015...if any. Approximately 390 Vietnam Veterans die every day, so in 2,190 days from the time of this writing, only six years, you'll be lucky to see a Vietnam Veteran still alive.

These statistics were taken from a variety of sources to include the VFW Magazine, The Public Health Office and the HQ CP Forward Observer 1st Recon., April 12, 1997.

The day I went to Vietnam I became a part of history and of a Brotherhood, as well. There wasn't a welcome home parade for any of us when we returned, but our Brothers in Arms were here waiting for us with a hug, a "Welcome Home Brother" greeting and the respect for a job well done, no matter what it was.

I'm proud to say I am a member of a three-patch motorcycle club known as In Country Vietnam Motorcycle Club (ICVMC). "We are a one-generation dinosaur MC, meaning, when the last Brother dies, so dies the patch." All of our Brothers are 100% pure In Country Veterans having been awarded the Vietnam Service Medal, validated

on each members DD-214 and we are known as The Dying Breed. Our motto is, "Vets Helping Vets". I recently attended our yearly national meeting, which was celebrated in Trussville, Alabama this past September of '09. Those of us from Minnesota included Springer, our MN State President; Beano, our HQ Chapter President; along with Road Kill, Southern MN St Lt from MN II Corps Chapter; Farmer, IA State President and National Sgt At Arms; Wing Nut, HQ Chapter Treasurer; Wolf, Northern MN State Lt from MN I Corps Chapter; Hack a.k.a. Dennis, and yours truly, Lucky, both from the MN HQ Chapter. Duppy, one of our Brothers, the Sr. MN State Lieutenant and State Chaplain, regrettably was unable to make this ride due to electrical problems with his bike. Duppy was my sponsor during my Prospect time with the club and next year I'm hoping we'll have a chance to ride together for our next annual national meeting.

Our trip was full of twists and turns, ups and downs, and a few bends that we weren't expecting. We had breakdowns, engine fires, empty gas tanks, and often the external weather didn't always match up with the internal weather. With the way things were going, Murphy's Law must have been riding bitch with the club on this trip. Our mishaps along the way were like the imperfections of a human being that express our individual character.

Every ride is different and there is something unique about it that always stays in your head. All I can say is "What a rush when you're doing 70 MPH in a blinding rainstorm and your only sense of direction is the small red dot of a taillight in front of you." The art of controlling a machine that's a lot bigger and more powerful than yourself can be a life changing experience that, at times, can give you your life back. Having all that power under your ass at your disposal can be a real shot in the arm for your self-confidence, especially in these kinds of weather conditions. Eight of us arrived dripping wet and safely to our destination in Alabama, and returned home to our families and friends just as safe and unfortunately, just as wet.

Over the years, I have thought of those I served with during the war. It's good to know I can visit them often because they are always in my heart and in my dreams. If I die out here on this bike doing what I love, my only hope is that my Brothers who have passed before, again will be waiting for me with a hug, a "Welcome Home Brother" greeting, a cold beer, and the respect for a job well done.

LLRB, Lucky

A Very Special Acknowledgment

I would like to extend a very personal and heartfelt thank you to some very special people who helped me during the process of writing this book. Because of your generosity and kindness, my dream of becoming an accomplished writer has become a reality.

With much appreciation, thank you to:

Mike Abeln	Scharline Olson
Mark Abeln	Eddie Rediske
Ererika Brown	Bruce Reyer
Bryan	Ashley Ross
Evan Cook	Jack Ross
Jean Dickerson	Nancy Ross
Bernie Dickerson	Sue Shingledecker
Stoja Dzaferovski	Ian Skemp
Becky Fredricks	Jim Slattery
Tami Haines	Julio Sotillo Rodriguez
Gayle Herseth	Sarah Sotillo Rodriguez
Colleen Hendrickson	Laurie Stein
Jerry Huffine	Bill Stevens
David Hamilton	Vickie Swanson
Travis Johnson	Darin Szabo
Jerry Kingren	Eric Voge
Chuck Koon	Thomas Vogel
Alfred Minniti	David Wilson
Bill Mock	Christopher Williams
Dennis Olson	Leyla Yunis

N·O·T·E·S

N·O·T·E·S